# VW Bus

## LAURENCE MEREDITH

SUTTON PUBLISHING LIMITED

Sutton Publishing Limited
Phoenix Mill · Thrupp · Stroud
Gloucestershire · GL5 2BU

First published 1999

Copyright © Laurence Meredith, 1999


*Title page picture*: A Microbus with sealed-
beam headlamps, early 1960s.

**British Library Cataloguing in Publication Data**
A catalogue record for this book is available from the
British Library.

ISBN 0-7509-2201-X

Typeset in 10.5/13.5 Photina.
Typesetting and origination by
Sutton Publishing Limited.
Printed in Great Britain by
Ebenezer Baylis, Worcester.

# ACKNOWLEDGEMENTS

The author is grateful to Julian David, Tony Booth, Phil Shaw and the curator
and staff at the Volkswagen Museum, Wolfsburg.

Launched in 1950, the uniquely styled Panelvan gave rise to four generations of classic
Volkswagen Transporters.

# CONTENTS

# INTRODUCTION

In the same way that the French produce the world's greatest wines, the English the best writers of fiction and Austria the most talented composers of music, the Germans build the best motor cars. The latter is no surprise; the first true motor car was invented and built in Germany and this country's automotive products still reign supreme in terms of engineering integrity, if not in styling beauty.

Daimler-Benz, BMW, Porsche and Volkswagen – I do not include Ford or Opel, because these concerns are American owned – have consistently led other car makers in the fields of engineering innovation, engine performance, economy and safety. All four established companies have always been one or more steps ahead of rivals, and responsible for the creation of many classic and desirable designs over the years.

Porsche's success in sports car racing became so monotonous between the 1960s and present day that the sport's governing body has sought to change rules and regulations on several occasions to give others a chance of winning. The sporting divisions of Daimler-Benz and BMW have likewise been hugely successful in motor racing, largely due to their leadership in the field of engineering innovation and commitment to excellence.

Volkswagen has excelled with production vehicles; the Beetle and Transporter are just two examples, although in recent times the Golf shows every sign of becoming even more successful than the 'insect' it spiritually replaced. This book is about the many generations of Transporter, a vehicle that came about in unlikely circumstances. From a pencil sketch in 1947 through to the sophisticated and powerful Buses of the late 1990s, the Type 2 utility vehicles have consistently been a benchmark by which all others of their ilk have been measured.

With their dependable, durable, rear-mounted, flat-four, air-cooled engines, the first three generations made between 1950 and 1982 have become the subject of a huge and growing 'cult' with a worldwide following. There are many reasons for this, and no single explanation is satisfactory or paints an entire picture.

Beyond its practical usefulness, proven reliability, ability to keep going on the most difficult terrain when conventional vehicles would have long since given up, immense strength and ruggedness, the classic Bus always has more to offer. Probably above all it has charisma, often described by enthusiasts in terms of an 'automotive soul' with which people can readily identify.

These vehicles have also provided a sense of the unorthodox in an automotive world that has often been wanting in character. By definition, convention is acceptable for the majority of folks but has rarely featured in the vocabulary of Volkswagen people.

In recent years classic Buses have been targeted by Volkswagen devotees in thousands, if not hundreds of thousands. These vehicles, taken for granted at one time, are now regarded as having made a valuable contribution to both the automotive and social history of the twentieth century. As a result, thousands of examples have been restored to as new, or better than new, condition and used with undisguised pleasure by increasingly enthusiastic owners.

There are owners' meetings in almost every country throughout the course of every year, and the 'scene' continues to grow. All this may be the result of nostalgia, an in-built human weakness, or strength, depending upon your point of view, but it certainly does no harm.

VW Buses are fun, interesting and its 'box on wheels' styling as conceptually valid in our modern age. Having been a fan of classic Volkswagens for more than forty years, I make no apology for expressing views in the text that follows which many will doubtless consider to be the result of bias and prejudice.

I have owned German vehicles all my adult life, enjoyed the benefit of having driven the automotive products of many other nations and concluded that air-cooled, rear-engined Volkswagens to be the best of the lot by a very wide margin. There is nothing else like them. Prejudiced and biased I might well be, but there are good foundations and explanations for both.

Without a rear bumper until 1953, the Transporters made up until 1955 were nicknamed 'Barn Doors' after their huge, top-hinged engine lids.

# Vehicle Chronology

| | |
|---|---|
| **1947** | Dutch Volkswagen importer, Ben Pon, sketches outline for a Panelvan |
| **1949** | Eight prototypes are successfully completed and tested |
| **1950** | First production Panelvans and Kombis are delivered to dealers' showrooms |
| **1951** | Range-topping Microbus de luxe, or Samba, is introduced |
| **1952** | The Single-cab Pick-up is debuted and proves popular with the building trade |
| **1955** | Revisions across the range include a roof 'peak' and a separate tailgate and engine lid to replace the 'barn door' |
| **1956** | Transporter production is transferred to a new purpose-built factory at Hanover |
| **1958** | The six-seater Double-cab Pick-up is debuted |
| **1959** | Redesigned engine is to the same configuration but power is increased from 30bhp to 34bhp |
| **1960** | The 600,000th Transporter rolls off the Hanover assembly lines |
| **1963** | The Type 3 saloon's more powerful 42bhp 1500 engine is available at extra cost |
| **1964** | 1500 engine is fitted with a throttle governor to curtail engine performance |
| **1965** | 1200 engine is discontinued; Italian Transporters are fitted with the newly introduced 1300 engine. Type 147 German post office van debuted |
| **1966** | Transporters are fitted with 12-volt electrics as standard, twelve months ahead of the Beetle |
| **1967** | 'Splittie' production ends and gives way to the revised 1600 Bay-window model |
| **1968** | Volkswagen celebrate production of the 2-millionth Transporter, while Westfalia completes the 30,000th Camper |
| **1970** | Front disc brakes are introduced along with twin-port cylinder heads |
| **1971** | Twin-carburettor, 1.7-litre engine is introduced |
| **1972** | All 1.7-litre models have the option of three-speed automatic transmission |
| **1973** | 1.8-litre engine debuts; US versions are fitted with Bosch fuel injection |
| **1975** | New range of LT commercials begins production at Hanover; regular Transporters are fitted with 2-litre engine |
| **1976** | Volkswagen celebrate production of the company's 30-millionth vehicle |
| **1978** | LT commercial is fitted with a six-cylinder diesel engine |
| **1979** | Bay-window Transporter production ends; the third generation 'Wedge' debuts |
| **1980** | Diesel-engined Wedge Transporter is officially announced |
| **1981** | Volkswagen's factory in Argentina begins Transporter production |
| **1982** | Wedge production continues but with a water-cooled flat-four engine in the tail |
| **1989** | Modern front-wheel drive Type 4 Transporter goes into production |
| **1999** | Bay-window Transporter production continues in Brazil |

# SKETCHY BEGINNINGS

*From 1950 to the present day there have been four successive generations of Volkswagen Transporters, each more generously proportioned than the last. The latest sophisticates with front-wheel drive and a wide variety of powerful engines are a far cry from the first model, the crude and austere Split-screen. The Volkswagen 'box on wheels', as the company's first chief executive, Heinz Nordhoff, once described it, is the most successful vehicle of its kind, often copied, but never bettered.*

# INTRODUCTION

The idea of a Dutchman and brought about principally by a Yorkshireman, the Volkswagen Transporter was borne out of necessity. A simple utility vehicle, but constructed to the highest standards, it stands alone in the world of commercial vehicles as a classic and enduring design.

The Bus was not only the first of a new breed but by far and away the best and most dependable. With the benefit of hindsight its birth and subsequent development, through several generations, was inevitable, although no one had even thought of such a concept until two years after Beetle production finally got under way in August 1945.

In 1947, or possibly as late as 1948, Holland's Volkswagen importer, Ben Pon (the first Volkswagen dealer outside Germany), made one of many visits to Volkswagen's factory in Wolfsburg. Pon was a perspicacious man who lived life to the full and, among other things, went on to enjoy a degree of success racing Porsches during the 1960s but, like so many of his generation, was thoroughly down to earth and a practical thinker. Also a good businessman, Pon rarely missed an opportunity.

In the aftermath of the Second World War, restoration of normal economic activity was a necessarily slow process. That any trade was able to continue was remarkable in itself but, such is the nature of the human spirit, it did. In Holland tradespeople – window cleaners, newspaper delivery people, carpenters and others – were inevitably short of motorised transport. The more fortunate ones had primitive three-wheelers and Pon was inevitably familiar with such strange vehicles.

On his critical visit to Wolfsburg, Pon observed a couple of even more unusual vehicles. To this day these have never been given an official name, principally because they were 'nailed' together from sundry bits and pieces that happened to be lying around the factory floor at the end of the war. These included Kübelwagen chassis, 1,131cc 25bhp Beetle engines, a flat bed constructed from metal and wood, a makeshift, rear-mounted cab and four wheels of dubious origin.

These flat-bed trucks were used as 'mules' for moving bits and pieces around the factory and proved most useful, if not, invaluable. One example continued to be used well into the 1990s because, like most simple inventions, a superior replacement had not been found. It was part of the Wolfsburg 'furniture' and no one had thought about driving it into the Auto Museum a little way from the factory, where it so richly deserved a permanent resting place.

When Pon spotted these he immediately thought of the tradespeople in his own country. To Pon, providing them with a more suitable mode of transport not only had possibilities, but was pressingly inevitable, blindingly simple and, above all, most urgent. Nothing elaborate was required.

In his mind Pon envisaged a Panelvan – a 'box on wheels' as Volkswagen's chief executive Heinz Nordhoff once dubbed it – and discussed his idea with Major Ivan

Hirst, who was in charge of the ownerless factory after the war. Now in his eighties, Ivan Hirst is one of the truly great men of the twentieth century, although very modest about his achievements. An intellectual, but unusually possessed of tolerance, patience and the capacity to understand another's point of view, even if it differed wildly from his own, one of Hirst's great strengths was his ability to listen and learn.

Hirst, whose family were business people, listened attentively to Ben Pon. The Dutchman's idea for a commercial vehicle made a great deal of sense but the development of a production version was not entirely in Hirst's hands. Had it been left to this young army major, a van would have come into being sooner than it actually did. There was, unfortunately, a stumbling block.

Permission for such a major project was required from Colonel Charles Radclyffe, who was in overall charge of light engineering in the British occupied zone of Germany. The British Army had regulations about such matters, and 'rules is rules'. Radclyffe was very much in the Hirst military mould but more cautious and ever-mindful of his duty to account to those both above and below him in rank.

After a good deal of fastidious procrastination, Radclyffe rejected Pon's idea, as the colonel correctly argued that there were not sufficient resources. Beetle production took priority, and it had not escaped Radclyffe's attention that there were large numbers of POWs employed at the factory, working long hours in pitiful conditions without very much to eat. Hirst respected his superior's opinion, relayed the message to Pon and the project died, albeit temporarily, there and then.

This was a great pity because, in theory, the Beetle's mechanicals were there for the taking. In principle the construction of a Panelvan only required extra consignments of sheet steel for the bodywork, but resources such as these had already been stretched almost beyond breaking point to keep pace with Beetle production. And the Beetle – a crude, noisy motorised 'soundbox' until the advent of the Export model in 1949 – needed to be refined before other projects could be undertaken.

However, the idea of a Beetle-based van would not go away. During his first meeting with Ivan Hirst, Ben Pon had drawn an outline pencil sketch of a Panelvan on a piece of scrap paper. Rough as this drawing appeared to be, it bore an uncanny resemblance to the first prototypes and subsequent production models.

The turning point for this stillborn project was Heinrich Nordhoff's appointment as Volkswagen's chief executive from 1 January 1948. The 'no-nonsense' ex-Opel executive had had the Pon sketch brought to his attention. Hirst had recommended Nordhoff's appointment; he was, in Ivan's words, 'the right man for the job'. The army major was not fond of Nordhoff's manner, but personal opinion played no part in army life when there were important jobs to be done.

After the German currency reforms of 1948, and exports of the Beetle to various European countries had begun, Volkswagen's infrastructure was slowly, but firmly established. Money earned from exports provided the possibility of investment in new projects; the Hebmüller and Karmann Cabriolet Beetles were targeted as the earliest models to expand the Volkswagen range.

But luxury, leisure-orientated convertibles were hardly a necessity when Germany's tradesfolk were carrying shovels, ladders and lunchboxes on prewar bicycles that had seen better days. Funds were tight but Hirst and Nordhoff pressed ahead and made the Panelvan a reality.

Draughtsmen in Wolfsburg's experimental department were ordered by Nordhoff to draw up plans for the production of a handful of prototypes. This work was completed in a matter of weeks and appeared to be so simple that all those involved genuinely wondered why the idea had not been put into practice many years earlier.

As a basis for the vehicle a standard Beetle platform chassis, with its integral and inherently strong steel 'backbone', was bolted directly underneath the all-steel Panelvan bodywork. Suspension front and rear was identical to the Beetle's, with transverse torsion bars and parallel trailing arms front and rear. The well-proven 1,131cc, 25bhp, flat-four engine was bolted to the four-speed, Porsche-designed, non-synchromesh gearbox, and slung into the tail out of harm's way. At all four corners were the Beetle's five-bolt, 16-in diameter wheels shod with the inevitable Continental crossply tyres.

The first prototype seemed to contain all the ingredients for a successful future. However, several test drives later it proved to be almost, but not quite, a complete catastrophe. That platform chassis was fine for the Beetle, but clearly was not strong enough to cope with the weight of the Panelvan. It buckled and creased in all directions and that first prototype soon became an undrivable pile of scrap, which was a pity.

However, a valuable lesson had been learnt; a stronger chassis was needed and would solve the problem. Back at the company's drawing board, the engineers devised a new affair, confident that the mechanical components – engine, brakes, gearbox and suspension – were perfectly adequate to the task ahead.

The new chassis was a conventional, sturdy steel structure with two parallel longitudinal box-sections, crossmembers and outriggers to support the outer extremities of the bodywork. To improve torsional rigidity, the ensemble was welded directly to the floor panelling and upper bodywork, making for an immensely strong semi-unitary-construction structure.

No more than eight prototypes were built and tested during 1949, and appropriate changes were made to improve these vehicles. The fuel filler, for example, originally placed on the outside of the rear bodywork, was relocated inside the engine compartment on the left-hand side. The pedals were also more conveniently spaced, the brakes improved and the front axle reinforced.

With a top speed of about 50mph (80kmh), the van's 'top-end' performance was within acceptable limits but acceleration was dismal, especially with a maximum ¾-ton load on board. This problem was satisfactorily and cheaply addressed by the incorporation of reduction gears – twin gear wheels that reduced overall gearing to aid acceleration – in the rear hubs. There was nothing new about these in a Volkswagen; they had been used in Porsche-designed vehicles during the war and Volkswagen simply drew on past experience for the production vehicles.

The eight prototypes comprised six Panelvans, Kombi (the 'entry-level' people carrier) and Microbus, and all acquitted themselves well in testing. Unlike the exhaustive and complex tests carried out on prototypes by today's manufacturers,

Volkswagen's methods at this stage were simple and comprised driving the vehicles for thousands of miles. If something broke it was strengthened.

If a component was shown to be wanting in any way, the experimental shop simply redesigned it – in a matter of hours, or even minutes – the workshop boys made it and production staff fitted it. There were no committees to answer to, no endless board meetings with presentations on 'flip-charts' and no accountants raising questions in the background. These were 'hands-on' mechanics and engineers getting the job done. If only their modern counterparts would learn from such a wonderful example.

The prototypes were easily equal to their intended job, and Volkswagen's people had every reason to be pleased that they had not only solved the problems of the first vehicle but had made a perfectly practical load carrier for the benefit of commercial tradespeople. Although they did not know it at the time, they were also on the brink of changing the world of commercial vehicles.

From 12 November 1949, when the first Panelvans were shown to journalists, through to their official launch in March 1950, no other vehicle of its kind would have such a large impact in its field. To reiterate, this was all due to a primitive sketch on a piece of scrap paper that took less than two minutes to draw.

From the first 'load-lugging' vans, a whole family of vehicles was devised, including the famous people carriers and 'hybrids' that would go on to be used for practically every conceivable function. Like its closely related sister the Beetle, the Transporter, Bus or Type 2, to give it its officially designated title (the Beetle was the Type 1), was developed over a long period of time and improved as a result. Fundamentally, its basic design did not change for many years.

The classic air-cooled vehicles lasted through three generations right up until 1982. Of these the Split-screen, or 'Splittie', era was pushed right up until 1967 and halted after the production of no fewer than 1.8 million vehicles. The Bay-window model that followed was a hugely improved vehicle, even though it was without much of the innate character that had endeared the original vehicle to so many. Despite this, it is the Bay model that forms the backbone of the thriving Volkswagen Transporter movement today.

This model was superseded by the Wedge in 1979, another fine rear-engined, air-cooled masterpiece, albeit a very different one from those that had gone before it. However, by 1982 when this model took its final bow, the principle of an engine and gearbox at the rear, the weight of which was balanced by cab passengers up front, was not entirely lost.

The modern range, produced from 1982, continued with this same format until the late 1980s. The engine was water cooled, gave considerably more power than the air-cooled engines of the traditional era and was an inevitable move on Volkswagen's part. A lack of engine performance had been the classic Bus's weakest, and most criticised, point.

It is not at all difficult to appreciate the reasons for these vehicles having developed such a wide 'cult' following, almost from the earliest days. Manufacturers like Daimler-Benz and Fiat produced similar vehicles – the Mercedes was every bit as good as the Volkswagen – but none captured the imagination of enthusiasts to the same extent as the VW Bus. The simple beauty of the Volkswagens, apart from their practical advantages, would ensure that the famous V-over-W motif would reign supreme and, in some respects, modern front-wheel-drive derivatives still do.

The latter are very different vehicles from their forebears – the Sharan is closer to the original concept – but are arguably appropriate for the 1990s. It remains to be seen as we go to press in spring 1999 whether Volkswagen will launch a 'Splittie' 'retro-clone', as the company has done with the Beetle. If it does, the whole cycle will undoubtedly start all over again.

Some things, like the zip, Dom Perignon vintage Champagne and the VW Bus, cannot in principle be improved. The basic design of the Transporter sits in the same hallowed company as the best of simple inventions, which is why survivors from the classic air-cooled period are being skilfully restored by enthusiasts the world over. Their efforts are huge, essential, in some ways senseless (thankfully) and to be applauded by all who like to live a little in an age that has long since disappeared.

Flat-bed trucks based on Kübelwagen chassis were used from 1945 to transport components and equipment around the factory at Wolfsburg, and gave Dutchman Ben Pon the idea of the truck for all trades. Interestingly, the caption on the rear of this rare archive picture dates this scene to 1960, which cannot be remotely accurate. These vehicles were still in use at the factory in the mid-1990s, but this example is wearing a robust set of Michelin radials with a tread pattern straight out of the 1970s.

The rear view of the truck is as bleak as it is from any other angle – hardly a styling masterpiece – and the battered Split-window Beetle bodyshell, possibly a victim of crash testing such as it was during the 1940s, equally so.

A flat-bed truck and a modern forklift truck working side by side, 1970s. Both were indispensable and unattractive, but were not improved in design for many years.

Although the flat-bed trucks were normally fitted with an enclosed cab, the driver of this laughably simple device worked alfresco. Here, the front torsion-bar springing and rear trailing-arm suspension are clearly visible. The 'nipple' type hubcaps are Beetle items from the early days

of production after the Second World War. Headlamps were fitted across the 'range', proof of the increasingly busy nightshift at Wolfsburg.

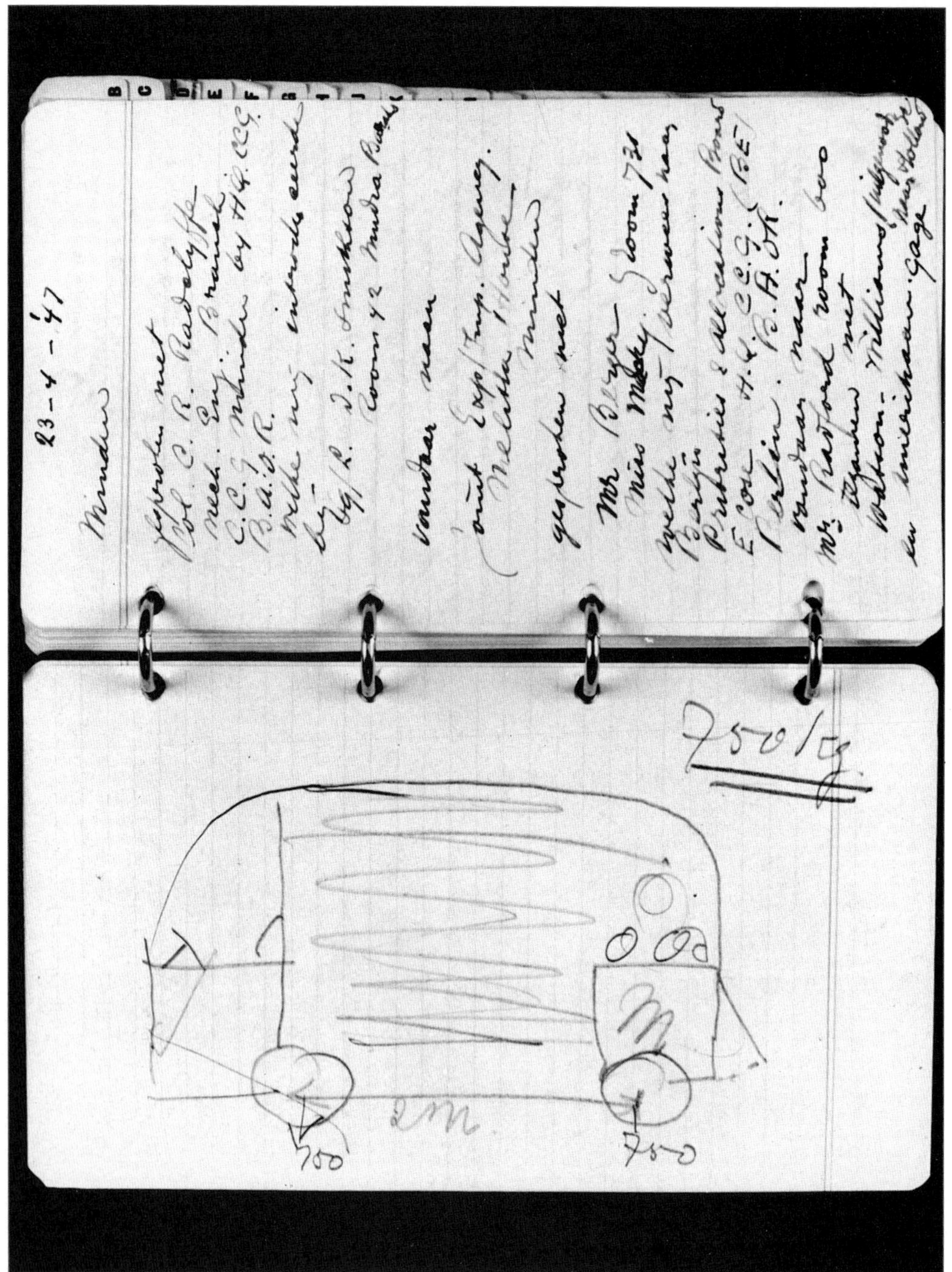

Ben Pon's simple sketch of a Panelvan took less than two minutes to draw in 1947, but bore a striking resemblance to the production vehicle launched just three years later. The notes in English on the opposite page are not particularly interesting, but the classic copperplate writing, taught in British schools until the 1970s, was a hallmark of a decent school education.

Major Ivan Hirst, now retired and living in Yorkshire, was instrumental in getting the Volkswagen Transporter into production. Without his efforts, the vehicle might not have arrived at all. During 1947, when Ben Pon called for these vehicles to be built, the Wolfsburg factory was stretched to meet demand for Beetles but Hirst pushed the Bus project through to its conclusion before leaving Wolfsburg in the 1950s to work for the Organization for Economic Co-operation and Development in Paris.

This fabulously well preserved 1949 Panelvan was just one of eight prototypes built in addition to the first vehicle that crushed and buckled its standard Beetle platform chassis. The headlamps, Y-shaped swage lines on the nose panel and front bumpers all conspire to create the visual illusion of a humble, happy, smiling face, and it was this above all other qualities that led to the vehicle's huge 'cult' following by the 1960s.

The definitive 1949 prototype Panelvan is without a rear window or rear bumper, the petrol filler is mounted externally and, like most prototypes from this period, the driver's door does not fit properly. Careful study of the side panels reveals the very low quality paint finish; this would be dramatically improved on production models, particularly after 1955. Note the diminutive tail-lamps.

Prototypes had heavy 'eyelids' around the headlamps, vertical engine-cooling louvres in the rear side panels and painted hubcaps. The V-over-W emblems in the centre of the hubcaps were sometimes, but not always, highlighted in a light colour. A most austere and basic vehicle, this example has just one windscreen wiper – for the benefit of the driver only.

Like the production vehicles, prototypes had semaphore indicators, a rear-view mirror mounted on the 'A' pillar, a 'contoured' front bumper and cab door handles standing proud of the sheet metal. This is how many older enthusiasts mostly remember the traditional Transporter and, although the 'Splittie' remained outwardly similar, it was subjected to many thousands of production modifications up to 1967 when it was superseded by the Bay-window model.

The well-used interior of a prototype Panelvan with paint kicked away from the steering column, a fair rip on the bench seat, scuff marks on the passenger's interior door panel and the rubber floor matting looking decidedly secondhand. However, these vehicles were never intended as rolling *objets d'art*, but the photographer might have considered removing the old rag from behind the seat before pressing the shutter button.

The prototype Kombi had luxurious rear seats – rather plainer on production versions – which were also removable to allow the vehicle to double as a load carrier. This facet of Kombi design was carried forward for many years. Like production 'Splittie' Kombis, the prototype was without a headlining and other luxuries, but customers never complained.

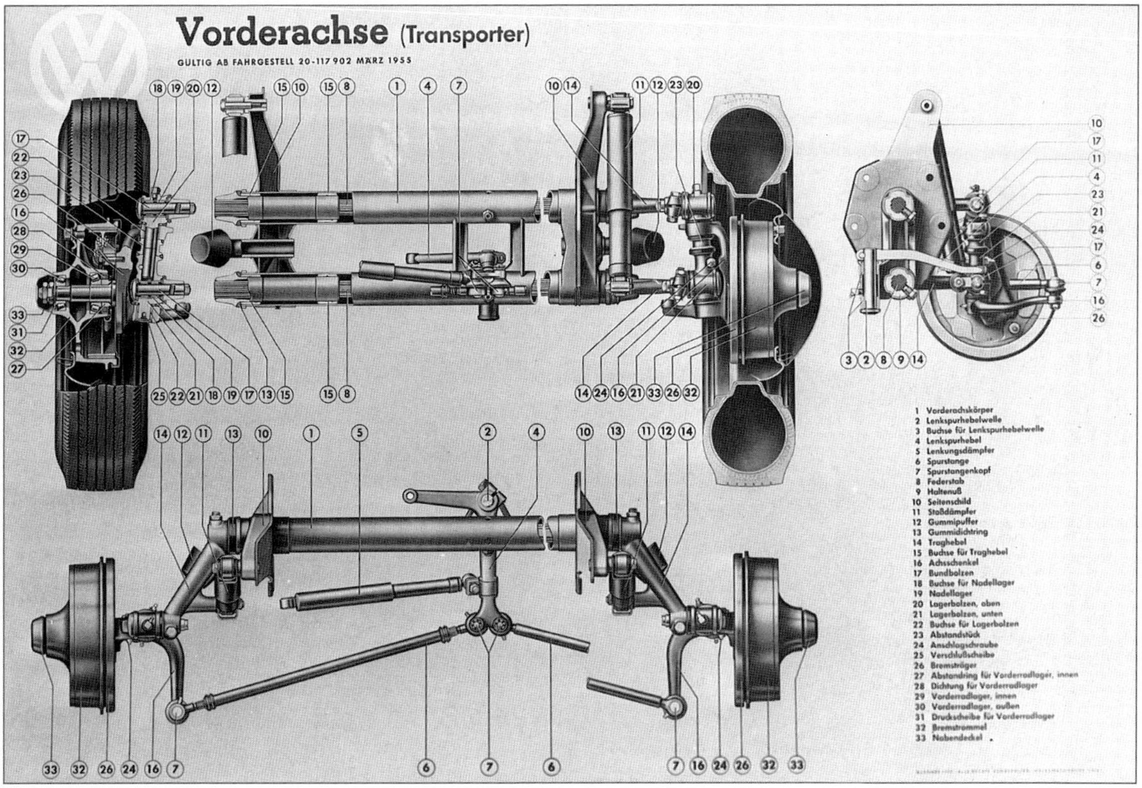

# Vorderachse (Transporter)

GÜLTIG AB FAHRGESTELL 20-117 902 MÄRZ 1955



Patented by Porsche's design office in 1931, torsion-bar suspension is undoubtedly the most durable springing medium ever devised. The Transporter's front assembly comprises a strong beam with torsion leaves running through the upper and lower tubes. A similar system was devised for the Beetle, prewar Auto-Union Grand Prix car, three examples of Britain's prewar ERA racing car, Karmann Ghia and many other Volkswagens. Steering is by unequal-length tie rods and articulation of the hubs by king and link pins.

A classic among classics, the horizontally opposed air-cooled engine is mated directly to the gearbox with just four bolts holding the two together. In this line drawing all major components can be seen, including the single camshaft below the crankshaft, Solex carburettor and inlet manifold, the all-important vertically mounted cooling fan above the engine and driveshaft from the gearbox. Casings for both the gearbox and engine were in light alloy; in this respect and many others the unit was light years ahead of its time.

The immortal Panelvan, launched in 1950, was the utility vehicle that changed the world of commercial vehicles. It was always crude and primitive, but there was nothing to equal its all-round versatility and it outsold the majority of its sisters in the range many times over.

# CHAPTER TWO

# BARN DOORS, 1950–5

*This early 1950 Panelvan was photographed for publicity purposes; it sports chromium-plated hubcaps, whereas the vast majority of those sold to the public had white painted items. Only the later luxury Microbuses were officially supplied with bright hubcaps, but the driver's expression suggests that he is not concerned about the sort of caps fitted.*

# INTRODUCTION

The first five years of production was critical for Volkswagen's future development of the 'Splittie' range. At the beginning Heinz Nordhoff had taken a brave gamble with what little hard cash was available for development purposes. Unlike the traditional British way – spend a fortune, make a fortune and fritter it away before grovelling to the government for handouts – Germans did, and continue, to do things very differently. Prudent housekeeping was an essential part of postwar Germany's economic thinking, and this was no more in evidence than at Wolfsburg.

The Panelvan had arrived in March 1950; people-carrying Kombis, which were little more than Panelvans with windows and removable seats in the rear 'cargo' area, and the slightly more luxurious Microbus debuted in June of the same year. In the design office it was known from an early stage that a pick-up truck would have been a useful addition, but it could not be afforded and had to wait until profits from the first models could pay for the development of one. In this respect, Volkswagen's policy was no different from that of an impecunious teenager delivering newspapers in order to save up for his first racing bike. The Bus had to pay its way.

Between 1950 and 1955 the 'Barn doors', as they have become known as a result of their enormous, top-hinged engine covers, were crude and austere, although exceptionally well made and gave good service. Many thousands were thrashed remorselessly and abused beyond reason, which is why there are so relatively few survivors, but commercial operators came to appreciate the Bus's inherent strength from an early stage. Sales increased steadily.

Until spring 1951 there was no back window and not even a rear bumper was made available for a further two years, but owners cared little about this. They had a vehicle capable of lugging large quantities of cargo, people (up to nine of them) or both, and this was not lost on taxi operators. The Kombi in particular was pressed into service as an almost unrivalled means of ferrying large numbers of people to and from airports, railway stations and the like – the more normal domain of the Mercedes-Benz diesel saloon.

Driving a Bus in these early days proved to be something of a novelty, especially for the journalists who tested them. Most found something they had not expected. The Bus drove a little like a Beetle, for the two vehicles shared many of the same parts, but the Bus was quieter because its engine was so much farther away from the driving seat, there was an integral heater built into the exhaust system – unusual for commercials at that time – and ride quality was exemplary. In short, it drove like a saloon car, albeit an underpowered and slightly heavy one.

The large 'split' windscreen, from which the Bus derived its 'Splittie' nickname, was large and gave a good view of the road ahead. There was a large diameter, three-spoke steering wheel similar in design to that of contemporary Beetles, and a single instrument – the speedometer – housed in a simple panel behind the wheel.

That the speedometer needle appeared to run 'backwards' was a charming feature made popular in the 1930s but wonderfully out of date by the 1950s.

There was cab bench seating for three – the separate driver's seat that Nordhoff had called for was not available until the early 1960s – and ribbed rubber matting on the floor. Kombis had seats in the rear attached to the floor with butterfly nuts; these could easily be unscrewed by hand and the seats removed so that the Kombi could be quickly turned into a load carrier.

The Kombi made for an ideal family vehicle. The plain vinyl upholstery was easy to clean, a great benefit to parents with children possessed of a propensity for travel sickness (as small children are apt to be), and more practical than the cloth upholstery fitted to Beetles of the same period.

This popular Kombi model was, of course, an 'entry-level' people carrier. But the Microbus was not that different. Apart from a headlining running the length of the vehicle and vinyl-clad interior panelling, in place of the Kombi's fibreboard panels, the Microbus was not exactly the luxury package that motoring folk might expect from a similarly named vehicle today.

However, journalists came to love the Transporter. Writing in *Commercial*, Laurence J. Cotton commented:

> In its entirety the 15cwt van is both remarkable in construction and performance, as I found during a series of tests, totalling over 200 miles in one day. Much can be said for the driving comfort in that I felt far from weary at the end of the run.
>
> Having previously driven a Volkswagen in Germany, its liveliness with light load was not surprising, but trying the van with a 15-cwt payload on home ground confirmed that it is speedy and economical, and well equipped, in its lowest ratio, to soar over the 1-in-4.5 gradient of Succombs Hill with power to spare.

Sales of Panelvans for 1950 topped 8,500 units, the majority sold only on the home market, and this was a paltry figure by comparison with Beetle sales but sufficient to maintain the degree of optimism Volkswagen felt necessary to make investment in future projects. The German economy was beginning to pick up and certain sectors of society were becoming affluent. To cater for this emerging middle class, Volkswagen launched the Sondermodell ('special model'), known popularly as the Samba, in April 1951.

The Samba was an instant success. The de luxe version of the Microbus, the Samba was indeed special and distinguished from other models by a number of different features. There was a full-length, roll-top sunroof, 'full-width' dashboard, chromed hubcaps, chunky alloy mouldings running along the flanks of the body and along the contours of the 'Y-shaped' swage lines on the front panel and improved interior panelling and upholstery.

In addition, there were wrap-around windows on the hind quarters, chromed luggage rails in the rear compartment above the engine and a series of four, rectangular 'skylights' on either side of the roof panel. The majority were finished in fashionable two-tone colours with red or 'coral' predominating as one of them.

This vehicle, above all, provided ordinary European middle-class families with their first opportunity of enjoying the freedom of foreign travel to exotic destinations on, for example, the Mediterranean coast, which certainly had not been possible before the Second World War. Americans, too, would eventually catch on, but it was not until the mid-1950s that Bus 'fever' struck the North American continent. Today, the Samba is arguably the most sought after of all Volkswagen Buses by collectors; Japan and America are the most popular destinations for original or well-restored examples.

During the first five years, production changes were relatively few and far between. The Beetle naturally took precedence, although, like the Beetle, the Transporter's 'crash' gearbox had synchromesh on the top three gears from 1952 and more engine power from 1953. The first of these changes was especially welcomed by those who had never mastered the skills of double-declutching and whose gear-changing efforts were characterised by irritating crunching and scraping.

In addition to these first three models, Volkswagen also produced an ambulance version from 1951. This differed most prominently from the regular models in that its rear barn door engine cover was hinged at the bottom. This was a simple measure to facilitate entry of stretcher-bound patients at the back. The two outwardly opening hinged doors on the side of the body (opposite the driver) made for awkward entry.

Ambulances were kitted out according to the specialised requirements of individual hospitals. Generally, they catered for one or two patients, two qualified medical staff and had shelving and storage space for surgical instruments, drips, bloodbags and other reminders of human mortality.

At about the same time Westfalia, the officially appointed camping converters, brought out the first of the famous 'Campmobiles'. Designed to sleep two adults and two children, Westfalias were generally among the best equipped and most thoughtfully laid out of all Campers. They were also the most expensive – but their example paved the way for dozens of other specialist converters in this lucrative field. All had sound but differing ideas about the concept of a motorised caravan.

As *Road & Track*'s testers noted:

> More a way of life than just another car, the VW Bus, when completely equipped with the ingenious German-made Kamper kit, can open up new vistas of freedom (or escape) from humdrum life.
>
> Many a car fancier will look down his nose at the bread box on wheels. It makes no attempt to be a high performance car. Acceleration is unexciting, curves and stops are best taken with all the time in the world, and even a glance at the photos will show you that the Kamper is top heavy. If you're a vacationer who likes to travel as far and as fast as possible, you'll have to change your habits to be moved much by this car.

The report concluded: 'The Kamper should be compared against car-and-trailer combinations, and in this contest it comes off well.'

In Britain the Devons, Dormobiles, Moortowns, Danburys and others would follow Westfalia's example and create a new way of life for many future generations. Campers were self-contained motorised maisonettes that doubled as a café, boardroom, bedroom, shooting lodge and general country retreat. They were relatively expensive, but well worth the extra money for those who spent their working lives in noisy factories and dreary offices.

Much of Volkswagen's publicity literature of the 1950s – now eminently collectable in its own right – had illustrations (water colours and photographs) of happy, smiling families travelling in their Buses through the snow-covered or sun-soaked peaks of the alps. The uncongested roads had an appeal all of their own and Transporter sales escalated, almost out of control, as a result. Volkswagen occasionally struggled to keep pace with increasing demand.

The introduction of the Pick-up truck in August 1952 only added to the working hours of production engineers. The Pick-up was an essential addition to the Transporter range. But its inception involved considerably more than 'slicing' the rear bodywork from a Panelvan and fitting a flat bed. A host of modifications were necessary, including relocation of a flatter fuel tank further forward and repositioning of the spare wheel from its shallow horizontal chamber above the engine to a purpose-formed well in the rear wall of the cab.

Engine-cooling louvres were cut into the side panels behind the rear wheels and inevitably a revised roof panel for the cab necessitated expensive retooling. With its folding side flaps and tailgate, locker-bed below the main bed and optional tarpaulin cover, the Single-cab Pick-up was an amazingly versatile vehicle and was used by many different trades for a huge variety of purposes. There were a number of variants on the Pick-up theme, dozens of special bodies and attachments for the agricultural, horticultural and service industries, and weird and wonderful gadgets for every imaginable application.

By the mid-1950s almost every country had discovered the Pick-up's aptitude for carrying heavy loads over long distances year after year without complaining. Unlike so many commercials, the Volkswagen was comparatively fast (conventional ambulances and fire appliances, for example, were relatively slow), comfortable and good to drive. Pick-ups and Panelvans sold in almost equal numbers, the former just edging ahead during the early years.

From December 1953 the range received a welcome boost in engine performance when the faithful 1,131cc, 25bhp flat-four was modified. By increasing the bore from 75 mm to 77 mm (giving a capacity of 1,192cc), increasing the compression ratio from 5.8:1 to 6.6:1 and valve diameters from 28.6 mm to 30 mm, engine output went up to 30bhp.

With these modifications the old-fashioned speedometer was changed for a more conventional unit in which the needle ran in the modern, conventional manner. The 60mph 'sprint' from rest could be achieved in a minimum of 75 seconds, a laboriously long haul, but it is as well to consider that many contemporary commercials were incapable of reaching 60mph, with or without a full load on board. Fuel consumption worked out at between 23–32mpg, and even if the vehicle was pushed up the steepest hills and most difficult roads for hours at a time it rarely fell below 20mpg.

Of the Panelvan, *Mechanix* magazine commented: 'You won't need a goat skin from the Beaux arts in Paris to realise this rig has the chic and boulevard appeal of a paratrooper's left boot or a pair of paint-splattered overalls. This is a purely functional workhorse and the designers obviously didn't give a damn whether it looked like an egg in a washing machine providing it did the work. And that it does.'

In 1954 the tail-lamps were redesigned and given a 'bubble-type' lens, rather than being flat as previously. However, the most important announcement that year was the planning of a new purpose-built factory at Hanover, specifically and exclusively for Transporter production.

Throughout this production period Wolfsburg had been a hive of frenzied engineering and design activity, which was aimed at preparing for sweeping changes to both the Beetle and Bus in 1955. Beetle production reached one million in this same year and was substantially modified. Likewise, the Transporter's character was dramatically altered and all these changes without exception were in the nature of genuine improvements. Volkswagen also launched the pretty two-seater Karmann Ghia sports car in 1955.

The Transporter vehicles made up to 1955 were utilitarian and basic, notwithstanding the superior appointments of the Samba model. Today, pre-1955 Buses are collectable and of great social interest but, by comparison with the vehicles made after March 1955, they are crude in almost every sense. Although the phrase MPV (Multi-Purpose Vehicle) had yet to be invented, this is what Volkswagen had succeeded so admirably in producing. It was early days but the future appeared to be a great deal brighter.

Resplendent in 'battleship' grey, early Transporters had 16-in diameter road wheels, skinny Continental crossply tyres and a large painted VW roundel on the front panel. Unlike modern vehicles, the removal of the VW badge on the 'Splittie' does not render the Bus unidentifiable. Restored to this condition today, these vehicles are almost worth their weight in gold.

Between the prototype and production model the fuel filler was moved from the external bodywork to the tank itself, necessitating entry to the engine compartment, which at least made those who habitually siphoned petrol think twice. A single exhaust tail-pipe sufficed until 1955, but the 'whacky' crossply tyres soldiered on and on until the 1970s.

Early Panelvans await despatch to dealers' showrooms, 1950. Devoid of rear windows and rear bumpers, these vehicles have painted VW roundels – the same items as those on the front panel – fitted where a small window would appear from 1951. Among the Export Beetles is a Standard model with painted hubcaps and chunky tyres, which illustrates that standardisation had yet to arrive in Wolfsburg on a large scale during these early days.

By 1951 the Panelvan had gained a rear window, although it was of dubious benefit when the cargo area was fully loaded. A rear bumper was added in 1953, but only if customers were prepared to pay extra for this 'luxury' item. At this angle the positive camber of the rear wheels, a feature of Beetles and Buses for many years, is shown to good effect. A degree or two of negative camber would have helped road-holding, but Buses were never intended to be Le Mans contenders.

A single brake lamp in the centre of the 'barn door' was hopelessly inadequate, even by the standards of the early 1950s, but saved Volkswagen money and complied with the company's 'minimalist' policy towards the utility Transporter. Note that the licence plate has been incorrectly drilled, a motor trade fault that continues in many cases to this day.

In the absence of a 'through-flow' ventilation system, fresh air was supplied through swivelling quarter-lights (not fitted to Beetles until 1952) in the cab doors, and fitted with a push-button integrated into the finger latch. The side windows were of the sliding variety to reduce production costs. There was nothing new in sliding windows – Land Rovers had had these since 1948 – but this did not stop BMC from hailing Alex Issigonis as some kind of genius for fitting them to the Mini in 1959.

Early Transporters had a throttle pedal resembling a beaver's tail; none of the pedals was covered with a rubber pad and often presented problems for drivers with wet, slippery boots. The workman-like handbrake lever (right) rises almost vertically from the floor; the steel bar in front of it is a foot rest for passengers. Note the style of the ribbed, rubber floor mat.

Disputes about early Transporter originality continue to rage among restorers. The generally held belief that 'Splitties' had white painted wheels is disproved by this early photograph taken at Wolfsburg. Three out of four have black wheels from which a general conclusion can be drawn that until standardisation in 1955, virtually anything was acceptable.

The large expanse of the Panelvan's steel bodywork lent itself well to signwriting, an important advertising medium for commercial operators. This well-restored example is a regular visitor to English Volkswagen shows.

The people-carrying Kombi was put into production in summer 1950 and was an inevitable addition to the Panelvan. This early Volkswagen studio picture, in which high-intensity lights and flashguns have been used, highlights both the body and interior. The detail depicted shows that the Bus was always considerably more than a 'box on wheels'.

Microbuses were much the same as Kombis, except that they had a better level of interior trim and, instead of having removable seats, the former's were fixed to the floor. The 'gap' between the floorpan and seat base on these, and the subsequent de luxe versions, was also closed with a vinyl-covered panel for neatness.

The oddments bin on the wall behind the cab seats was the preserve of Microbuses, although not on the earliest examples, and fitted with a chromed smoker's companion. After 1955 these vehicles could be ordered with a walkway between the driver and front passenger seats. Note the style of the coarse-weave carpeting in the rear and ribbed rubber matting on the floor.

Introduced in June 1951, the range-topping Microbus de luxe, or Samba, had a roll-top sunroof, glass skylights, wrap-around rear quarter windows and external brightwork very much in evidence. The most desirable of all the classic 'Splittie' Transporters, the de luxe usually came in fashionable dual-tone colours. Despite feeble performance from the original 25bhp flat-four, and subsequent 30bhp and 34bhp engines, concours examples are much sought after the world over.

In addition to the roof windows and wrap-around glass at the Samba's hind quarters, de luxe versions had four side windows in contrast to the regular people carrier's three. This 1955 example also has bright mouldings attached to the outsides of the engine-cooling louvres, which were considered as luxury touches in the 1950s.

The universally acclaimed Single-cab Pick-up truck originally debuted in 1952 and proved especially popular in the building trade on both sides of the Atlantic. Most of these vehicles led exceptionally hard lives, as did their owners, but both seemed almost to go on for ever. The cabs of all builder's

trucks always reeked of tobacco smoke, a smell with which the modern generation will not be quite
so familiar.

De luxe Microbuses were considerably more sumptuously appointed than the more basic models in the range. There were fluted vinyl seat covers, vinyl interior panelling conveniently fitted with passenger armrests and a soft-cloth headlining that extended to the roof pillars and metal panels at the base of the side windows. All of these features greatly increased the purchase price, but many thought the extra expense worthwhile. Probably the greatest benefit from such 'luxury' was the effect the vinyl side panelling and headlining had on supressing engine noise.

Large American saloons predominated on the streets of São Paolo, Brazil, in the 1950s. Volkswagen set up a manufacturing plant in this developing country as early as 1953. This pre-1955 delivery van appears ever so slightly humble against the newly built sky-scraping buildings but by the mid-1960s Volkswagens would become this country's most popular vehicles. Extraordinarily, second-generation Bay-window Transporters are still being made in Brazil in 1999!

Not a new method of transport in the twenty-first century – although this might not be a bad idea for easing road congestion – this early Kombi has been converted for rail use. Over the years Transporters have been used in a bizarre range of roles; rail transport was one of the more normal and safe of the alternative functions and had all but died out by the mid-1950s.

A mobile post office, which provided an excellent solution in remote rural areas where traditional post offices proved to be uneconomical, mid-1950s. This vehicle even has a modern stamp dispenser at the rear. History might repeat itself one day.

Primitive, simple and basic, pre-1955 Buses made life easy for all sorts of tradespeople. Large diameter 16-in wheels shod with perilously narrow crossply tyres, wholly inadequate semaphore indicators and poor all-round visibility were all part of the original Transporter package, but Germany in particular would not have been developed to the same extent without it.

# CHAPTER THREE

# THE SAME ONLY . . ., 1955–67

*A Kombi Transporter proudly displaying its revised rear at Wolfsburg, 1955. The huge barn door has gone, and a smaller engine lid and upper tailgate have taken its place. This was a much more sensible arrangement and a long time in coming, even if access to the engine was a little more restricted as a result.*

# INTRODUCTION

From March 1955 the Bus's frontal appearance was greatly improved by the addition of a 'peak' above the divided windscreen. This had the effect of adding to the Bus's frontal 'human facial' characteristics, but was also beneficial in a practical sense. In previous years customers had complained about inadequate interior ventilation – the Beetle's cabin was similarly insufficiently served until the advent of quarter-lights in 1952 – and Volkswagen took a long while to do anything about this.

Their solution was to cut an aperture, covered with metal gauze, in the underside of the roof peak, which directed fresh air into a rectangular steel distribution box attached to the underside of the cab roof. The rate of flow was controlled by a handle on the left-hand side of this box and was effective in keeping occupants of both the cab and rear passenger compartment cool – especially important in the hot summers of central Europe and California! It was a simple system and worked well.

All models received a 'full-width' dashboard – formerly the preserve of the Samba only – and this was of a more modern design. In addition to the speedometer, the Samba exclusively had a circular, dashboard-mounted clock from its inception. The replacement clock from 1955 was a great deal smaller, rectangular and not quite so imposing, but, of course, did the same job as previously. This was in spite of the fact that by 1955 the majority of Bus owners were content with obtaining the same information from the instrument they wore around their wrists.

The spare wheel across the range was housed in the cab in a specially formed well in the rear wall in the same style as the Pick-up three years earlier. At the rear, the barn door engine lid was dropped, and replaced with two smaller lids – one covering the engine compartment and a top-hinged tailgate above, which opened to give access to the rear luggage space over the engine. This was a far more sensible and convenient arrangement, even though it reduced the amount of space around the engine for maintenance and servicing purposes.

Other noteworthy changes included a decrease in the diameter of the road wheels – from 16 in to 15 in – which reduced unsprung weight (not noticed by owners), and an improvement in ride quality by the simple expedient of lessening the diameter of the torsion bars by 1 mm from 30 mm to 29 mm.

All of these changes were substantial and helped to sell more Buses. In the same year Heinrich Nordhoff's efforts were richly rewarded, not only by healthy profits but by the Braunschweig (Brunswick) Technical College bestowing an honorary professorship upon him. It was a great privilege of which he was justly proud.

By 8 March 1956, the first Hanover-built Transporter had rolled away from the brand-new production lines and the Suez Crisis was about to cause great problems. As a result of the latter, fuel rationing was introduced in several European countries, but this war – described diplomatically by the British government as an 'armed 'conflict', rather than war – was a brief affair and had no effect whatsoever on Volkswagen sales.

Beetles, Beetle Cabriolets, Karmann Ghias and Transporters were leaving dealers' showrooms at a hitherto unknown rate. By November 1957, the Hanover plant had produced no fewer than 300,000 Transporters since production had started there just a year earlier.

During the following three years or so, small improvements continued to be made to the range but in essence the Transporter remained much the same as it had been from March 1955. There were, however, significant additions to the range. The first of these was the wide-bed Pick-up in October 1958, available with either an extended metal or wooden bed to give extra carrying capacity. Just a month later the six-seater Double-cab Pick-up debuted and proved to be invaluable in all sorts of applications and industries from public service utilities to the many branches of the building trade. Although the Double-cab model was without the Single-cab's useful lower-deck locker-bed, generous storage space was provided below the seat in the rear of the cab, and proved useful for so many purposes.

In recent times the Double-cab vehicle has developed something of a 'cult' following of its own, particularly among younger people in Britain and the USA. Apart from being aesthetically interesting, it makes for practical, inexpensive family transport, although today many are highly prized concours exhibits and normally only seen at Volkswagen 'spit-and-polish' shows.

From May 1958 safety was also improved, as the rear lamps were provided with a brake light apiece to replace the single stop-lamp that had previously sat in the centre of the rear panel. A little later vehicles exported to North America were fitted with much larger, heavier front and rear bumpers. They had an upper bar above the main blade and passed through much taller overriders. Similar to the ones also fitted to the Beetle for the American market, these took into account the increasingly tight spaces in which motorists were expected to park, especially in urban areas. These bumpers arguably gave the Bus a rather heavy appearance, but the majority of owners considered them to be an aesthetic improvement.

Not to put too fine a point on things, several other manufacturers had 'noticed' the great success of the Volkswagen Transporter and pressed ahead with plans to make rival versions. Naturally, Detroit would make larger vehicles with much more powerful engines. One design after another came along, particularly in the early 1960s, but none was as successful as the Volkswagen for one simple reason.

By comparison, the VW Bus was slow, noisy and of rather humbler proportions, but rival designers had forgotten, or had not understood, the one absolutely vital facet of the VW that had endeared it to so many. Above all the VW Bus had a unique frontal appearance that, with a very 'human' countenance, appeared to smile. In various surveys over the years, people have consistently voted owls as their favourite birds – for the very same reason.

Detroit's offerings were unattractive and 'glittering', plastered in 'acres' of brightwork and of immodest gait. The Volkswagen was seen in some quarters as an underdog, and underdogs are often the real winners. By and large, Nordhoff and his team forged a single-minded path and simply ignored what the opposition were producing.

Despite press criticism that the Bus, and Beetle, would benefit from a more powerful engine, such pleas were also largely unacknowledged. In May 1959, the Bus engine was completely redesigned, although at first there was no gain in horsepower. It was made stronger, the cylinder barrels were spaced farther apart for improved cooling, and there was a new gearbox with one-piece 'tunnel' casing, instead of the two-piece affair of the previous years. Twelve months later an increase in compression ratio to 7.0:1 and a new Solex 28 PICT carburettor saw power increased from 30bhp to 34bhp. This was a poor gain – Volkswagen folk hailed these modifications as significant – and made comparatively little difference to performance out on the road where it mattered most.

One huge benefit of the fresh carburettor was the automatic choke that came with it. Some owners, particularly in the Beetle fold – which had been treated to the same modification – claimed that fuel consumption suffered as a result. However, this was incorrect, as road test results revealed.

Although they were not much faster, the 34bhp vehicles were better to drive. Their revised engines were smoother, generally more durable and, although unimportant, prettier in appearance. The detachable alloy dynamo pedestal was less conspicuous than the outgoing one, which had been cast integrally with the right-hand side of the crankcase.

During the early years of the 1960s the world began to change rapidly. Safety started to play an important part in the briefs of design and production engineers. The 'bullet-type' indicators on the front panel, for example, were seen as a potential threat to pedestrians, in much the same way as 'bull-bars' on four-wheel-drive 'Tonka Toys' are today.

As a result, these were changed for flat, circular items. American-spec vehicles received sealed-beam headlamps and these, in conjunction with the revised indicators, improved the Bus's frontal appearance. It became even more 'human'-looking. A fuel gauge was fitted in 1961, more than ten years after a number of customers had suggested that this item 'might' have been a useful addition to the dashboard.

At the same time the High-roof Panelvan was added to the range, the final model in the 'Splittie' line-up. These were wonderful vehicles used in large numbers by the German post office and members of the rag trade across the whole of Europe and North America, but less so in Britain. Many were also converted into mobile cafés, hairdressing salons, for example, because the extra height of the roof allowed for even the tallest people to stand upright.

In Britain at this time, Camper manufacturers were beginning to thrive and of all offerings the Devon range was the most popular. Caravettes and Torvettes were selling well at about £1,000 apiece, roughly £300 to £400 more than than the cost of a new Beetle, and proved ideal for family weekends away. Such was the novelty of these vehicles that most owners tolerated the discomfort caused by condensation rolling down the interior walls after each night's sleep with relish.

In 1961, Volkswagen debuted the first of several cars intended to replace the aged Beetle. This was the Type 3 saloon with a conventional three-box body. One of its greatest assets was its 1,493cc, 47bhp engine, which endowed it with 80mph-plus performance, and ought to have been slotted immediately into the tail of the Beetle.

Above all it would have silenced the Beetle's critics, many of whom habitually complained about the car's lack of performance. But it was not to be and it took Volkswagen until 1966 to be persuaded of the merits of the 1500 engine in the little car.

However, the Transporter was treated to the new power unit as early as 1963. At first it was only available in vehicles exported to North America, where Detroit's rival machines were gaining ground. The 34bhp 1200 version continued to be made available until 1965, but most customers opted for the more powerful engine which, on a good day, was capable of propelling the Bus up to 70mph, and beyond in some cases. This worried Volkswagen greatly.

The 1500 had improved brakes to cope with the extra engine power, but stopping a high-speed Bus was one thing – and stopping its load was quite another. To counteract the benefits of the 1500 engine, a throttle governor was fitted to the Solex carburettor at the start of the 1965 model year in August 1964. This spoilt everyone's fun, but not for too long. Many owners spotted this device and put a couple of the spanners in the vehicle's tool kit to good use and quickly removed it. A throttle governor, they argued, was ridiculous on a vehicle that developed just 42bhp, and they had a point.

With the 1500, Volkswagen remained at the top of the commercials' best-seller's lists. It was inexpensive to buy and run and, like the 1200, proved itself more than capable of running beyond the prescribed 3,000-mile service intervals. Some owners became so complacent about maintenance, that they gave up this chore altogether, usually with inevitable consequences. Volkswagens did not break very often but, when they did, repair bills were always likely to be high; this served as a warning to future generations of enthusiasts.

Technical improvements continued to be made year after year and were incorporated into the Bus at roughly the same time as the Beetle was also treated to modifications. Exhaust heater boxes were changed for heat exchangers in 1963 to avoid the possibility of exhaust fumes and oil odours, picked up from the engine, entering the cabin through the heater pipes. In recent years owners have voiced their discontent in no uncertain terms about the supposed inadequacies of the Bus's heating system. This is solely down to non-genuine heat exchangers being fitted.

In August 1963, there were more, somewhat insignificant changes. The engine cooling louvres on the outer bodywork were cut to face inwards, rather than outwards as previously – supposedly a safety consideration – and the road wheels were decreased in diameter from 15 in to 14 in. They continued with the same five-bolt pattern and, despite the advent of radials, were shod with Continental or Michelin crossply tyres which, of course, were as inadequate as ever.

From August 1965, the rear window on Panelvans and people carriers was increased in width, and improved rearward visibility, but in consequence the Samba lost its wrap-around rear quarter windows. This turned what had become known as the 23-window Samba into the 21-window Bus, an equally fine machine, but future generations would favour the former of these two range-topping vehicles.

Also in 1965, the 1300 engine was introduced and gave a welcome boost to flagging Beetle performance. This unit developed 40bhp – just 6bhp more than the

1200 – but only found its way into Transporters exported to Italy. The rest of the world bought 1500s in ever increasing numbers.

During this same year Volkswagen also brought out a new kind of Transporter, the Type 147 'Fridolin'. This was to a unique two-box design with the 1200 engine mounted in the tail and intended for use by the German and Swiss postal authorities. Much smaller than the regular Transporter, with a sliding door on each side, the frontal appearance was similar to the Type 3 saloon and had an interior completely devoid of creature comforts.

As an aside, Volkswagen had also completed the construction of a huge wind-tunnel facility by the end of 1965, which was a positive development, but begged the question as to why the K70 saloon, launched in 1970, had such poor aerodynamic properties.

By the mid-1960s, the 'Splittie' was well overdue for a replacement. It had enjoyed a long production run – not long enough for some – but a more modern Bus was required, a more 'up-market' vehicle to cater for the demands of increasingly affluent customers.

In August 1966, 12-volt electrics replaced the old and inadequate 6-volt system. This was a year before the Beetle was treated to the same upgrade and was a welcome change, but it was not enough to save the 'Splittie' from its inevitable production doom. In August 1967, a more sophisticated and much improved vehicle to a fresh design was announced and rapidly increased Volkswagen's profits.

From the front, Buses made after March 1955 were distinguished with a roof 'peak' over the top of the windscreen. This incorporated a gauze-covered vent for the newly introduced fresh-air system. With the long, roll-top sunroof open, the Samba did not want for further fresh air, but the new system was welcomed nonetheless. Many argue that the roof peak also improved the appearance of the 'Splittie'.

A crystal-clear illustration produced as a press handout in 1955, which shows the superior interior access afforded by the newly introduced top-hinged tailgate. It is reassuring for all those employed in motoring journalism that the photographer has forgotten to remove the aerosol can from the dashboard before pressing the shutter . . . the good ol' days.

Post-1955 Kombis were roughly to the same specification as they always had been but, unlike this example, the majority were finished in single body colours.

Whereas a full-width dashboard had formerly been the sole preserve of the de luxe Microbus, all Transporters had this item after March 1955. The radio in the centre of this example is modern, while the signpost reading lamp attached to the windscreen is a period accessory.

The Transporter's opening side doors provided excellent access to the interior but, being of the hinged variety that opened outwards, they were not particularly convenient in 'kerbside' loading situations. A single sliding door would have been a much better, although expensive, solution, but this was not introduced until the launch of the second-generation Transporters in August 1967.

Volkswagen never made a Camper version, the official conversion work being farmed out to Westfalia. These vehicles were relatively expensive but offered so many the freedom to travel during the 1950s and 1960s. Westfalia's Campmobile began a huge industry, British converters being among the most imaginative. The striped socks worn by the male model in this shot perfectly complement the Westfalia's dual-tone paintwork, but that haircut is straight out of America's wild west.

From March 1955 US-spec Transporters began to differ a little from European versions. From this time, the former were fitted with 'bullet-type' indicators on the front panel and had clear lenses. European vehicles would continue to be fitted with semaphore indicators until 1960, when they

too would have bullet indicators but with amber lenses. This Microbus also has sealed-beam headlamps, a legal requirement in North America in the early 1960s.

Heinz Nordhoff had called for a separate driver's seat as early as pre-production days but had been told in no uncertain terms that this was not technically possible, which is why a three-man bench seat continued in the cab after 1955. Nordhoff would eventually get his way, but not until 1961. This shot is interesting for the scene reflected in the hubcap; the photographer and his assistant are clearly visible, a fundamental mistake of many professional lensmen which, in some cases, is perpetuated today.

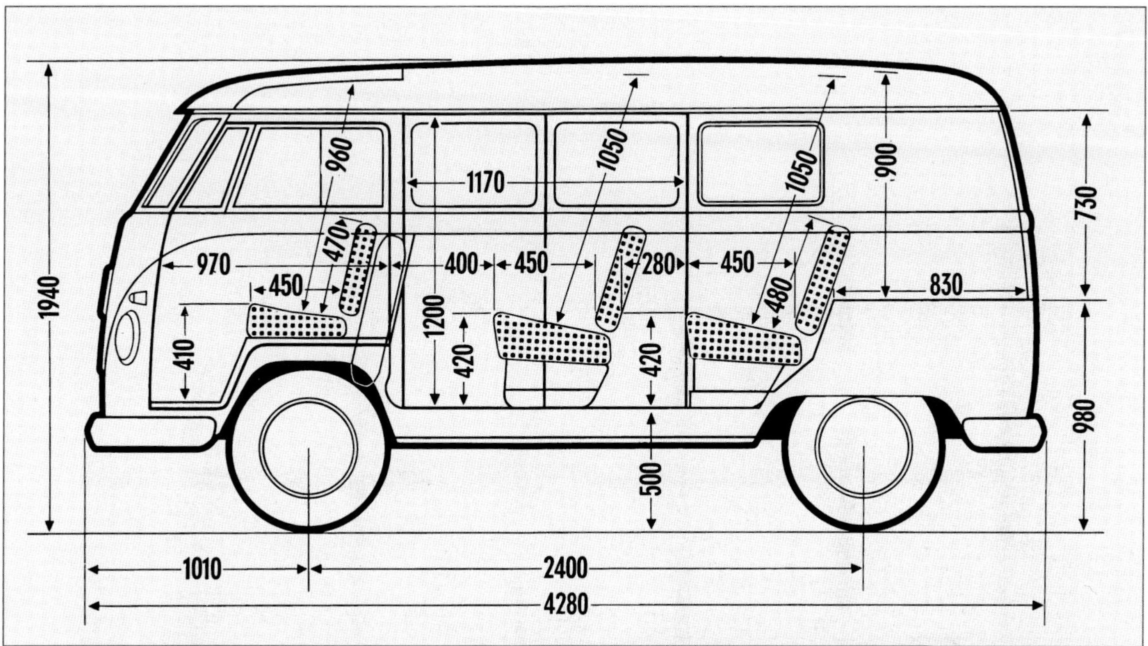

Line drawings like this were popularly depicted in Volkswagen's publicity literature, but it is doubtful whether the majority of potential customers (with the exception of fanatical enthusiasts) ever correlated measurements in millimetres with the space available. To Volkswagen's clientele these measurements were probably on the whole meaningless, but the draughtsmen loved producing such wonderful drawings.

By the end of the 1950s and early 1960s, each model in the range appeared to have been modified very little, but detail changes continued to be made. From 1958, the bumpers were larger and stronger, the external rear-view mirror had been mounted on the door hinge and door handles had been recessed into the sheet metal for safety.

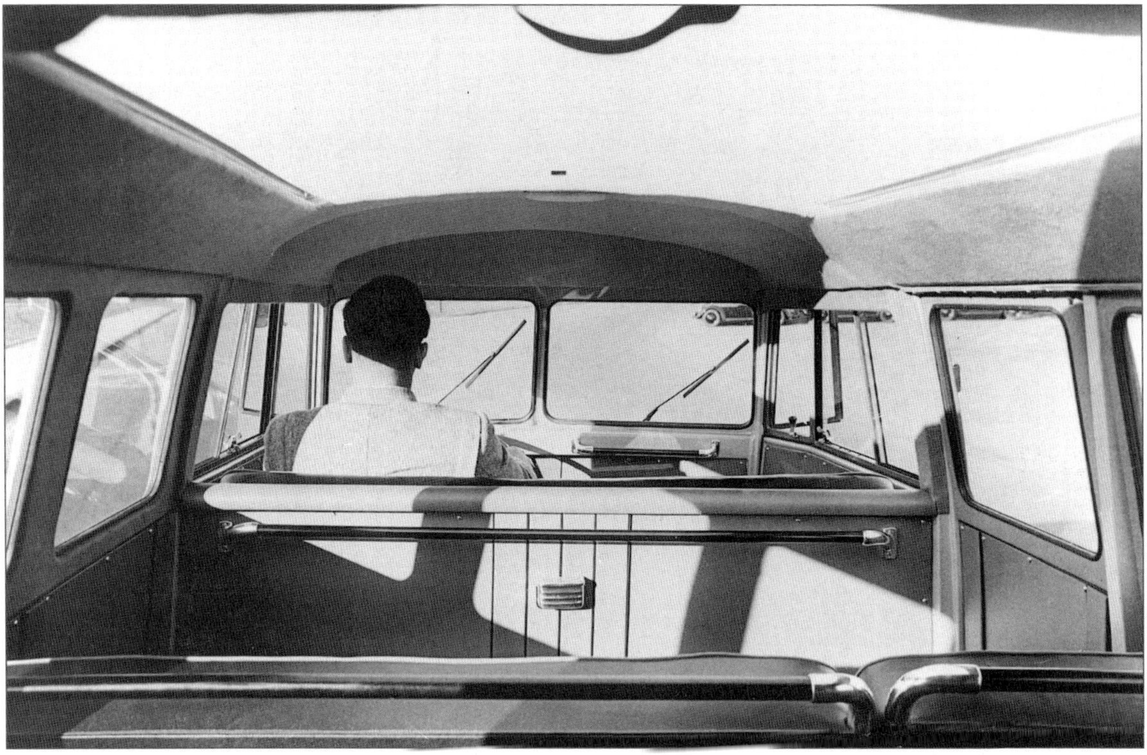

The interior of a pre-1955 Microbus is naturally spacious but fairly basic in appointments. Fitted here with the optional sunroof (standard on the de luxe version), there are also grab rails for passengers, but seat belts were not added until the 1970s. It is worth comparing this picture with the next one of a post-1955 Microbus.

As well as the full-width dashboard the post-1955 Microbus's interior is much more welcoming. There is still only one sunvisor – passengers got one at extra cost – but the newly introduced cabin ventilation system (featured across the range) can be clearly seen on the underside of the cab roof. This was little more than a metal distribution box, the flow of air being regulated by a handle on the left-hand side, but it worked well enough and was especially appreciated by rear seat passengers in hot weather.

Whereas Beetles during the 1950s had elegant cloth-covered seats, Buses had eminently more practical, easy-to-clean, vinyl upholstery. The backrest of the seat (left) of this Microbus tilts forward to ease entry to and exit from the rear. The vinyl side panelling and horizontal bright mouldings are typical of period decor.

Available from 1958, many regarded the heavy American-spec bumpers as aesthetic improvements; these were popular extra-cost options in non-US markets. Note that this Microbus, fitted with the optional roll-top sunroof, has a painted VW roundel on its front panel; de luxe Microbuses always had a chromed item.

The glorious Samba, or de luxe Microbus, was similarly unchanged in its external appearance for many years. This early 1960s example has bullet-type front indicators and rubber inserts on the front bumpers for enhanced protection.

Introduced in 1958, the Wide-bodied Pick-up truck was fitted with either a metal or wooden platform and could obviously carry much larger loads.

Also debuted in 1958, the six-seater Double-cab Pick-up, or Crew-cab, was a supremely versatile vehicle. Although without a locker-bed, there was a certain amount of storage space below the rear cab seat. Double-cabs would feature in all future Transporter generations and become popular in North America as family leisure vehicles.

Westfalia Campers – this one has its curtains drawn in daylight for reasons that are not readily apparent – were comprehensively equipped for family holidays. The roofrack is a period accessory but is not particularly reachable without a ladder. Yet another flawed publicity photograph, the photographer is clearly visible in the front hubcap.

By the mid-1950s Transporters like this Samba had colonised almost every country in Europe. They were ideal touring vehicles and provided thousands with their first opportunity to take an annual holiday in 'exotic' foreign countries.

A group of children having a lot of fun with a
23-window Samba in Paris, 1950s. These happy
looking youngsters were obviously and blissfully
unaware of the misery from which the
Volkswagen project grew. Just a few years earlier
the factory at Wolfsburg had been little more
than a bombed-out shell. By the time
Volkswagen's photographer had shot this, the first
2-million Beetles had been produced and such
was demand for Transporters that a new factory
at Hanover had started production by 1956.

From the early 1960s, this must rank as one of Volkswagen's most contrived publicity photographs ever. The
beautifully appointed Westfalia Camper was designed for two adults and two children – not quite 2.4 children –
and pointed in the direction of future middle-class social trends. It is difficult to imagine that the people in this
shot were actually enjoying their modelling assignment.

In this contrived Volkswagen publicity shot, a Heinz Nordhoff 'look-alike' is cooking a plastic fish over an unlit fire, while an 'over-dressed' woman gazes through a pair of binoculars at a couple of chivalrous chaps helping a young lady from a craft, also captured on film by the beachcomber on the right. The 23-window Samba is a subtle but powerful player in the background of this busy family scene. Is the man on the left trying to cool his finger in the wind after tamping down hot tobacco in his stylish pipe?

Introduced in 1961, the High-roof Panelvan was the last of the 'Splittie' range. A good many saw service in postal duties and were also used by members of the clothing trade. Some of these vehicles were also employed as mobile cafés and hairdressing salons. This example has a top-hinged side hatch, converted specially for the catering trade. Production High-roofs, incidentally, were almost always supplied with white-painted hubcaps.

By the early 1960s, the people-carrying Kombi had been 'noticed' by rival manufacturers, who attempted with varying degrees of success to capitalise on the MPV market. American manufacturers made versions with very much more powerful engines and greater interior space, but they had little effect on Volkswagen sales.

More silly grins, well orchestrated poses and an idyllic weekend scene in the German countryside signify contemporary photographic trends. The Bus driver is happier reading a newspaper; married to a woman who wears trousers like that, who wouldn't be? With its underpowered 30bhp, 1200 engine, it was travel in hilly countryside like this that drew most criticism about the early Buses. The Transporter needed more engine power, but the 1500cc version was not made available until 1963.

The High-roof's serving hatch is supported on a pair of sliding stays; the wooden serving ledge below simply folds down. As mobile cafés and libraries, these amazingly practical vehicles were

popular in both Europe and America, but less so in Britain. Rival manufacturers copied the design but the Volkswagen was the first and by far the best.

It is doubtful that Volkswagen's view of a typical family camping scene really included a conflagration of which an average pyromaniac would have been proud, and tents capable of housing a wedding party. The relaxed couple sitting at the dining table appear to be oblivious to the inferno. The Kombi is fitted with a roof-mounted luggage rack for extra carrying capacity. These were accessories available from Volkswagen dealerships but, packed with luggage, they had an adverse effect on the Bus's handling in crosswinds.

Intended as a replacement for the aged Beetle, the Type 3 saloon was launched in September 1961 and had a more powerful 1500 engine. The same engine found its way into the Transporter in 1963, but only in American-spec vehicles at first. In 1964 Volkswagen fitted a throttle governor to the Transporter's 1500 to inhibit its performance; many owners promptly removed these, but that was their choice.

As the 'bullet-type' front indicators were considered to be potentially dangerous to pedestrians, these units were changed for flatter, circular items on American-spec vehicles in 1961. European-spec vehicles were similarly fitted a couple of years later.

By the late 1950s and early 1960s, converted Panelvans like this were widely used in Germanic countries in all sorts of unlikely roles. No other vehicle was as useful, practical or versatile, nor quite so compact and elegant. What a pity that today's roadside mobile cafés are not quite so clean, refreshing or good looking.

A massive modern city founded largely on the fortunes of the Volkswagen factory, this scene is characteristic of Hanover in the 1960s. With its extending, hydraulically operated arm, the way this converted Pick-up truck is being used is also typical of the many diverse purposes for which Transporters were adapted. The buildings in the background are largely residential apartments for factory workers.

Although many modifications had been made to the range by the mid-1960s, in essence it remained the same as ever. This 1964 model is distinguished by a larger rear window, an amber segment for the indicator function in the rear lamp clusters and engine cooling louvres cut to point inwards, rather than outwards as previously. The 1200 engine was discontinued from the following year.

Because the rear window was enlarged in 1964, the top-of-the-range 23-window Samba lost its wrap-around rear quarter windows and promptly became known as the 21-window Samba. It was not quite as desirable for this reason. The classic two-tone colour schemes were popular until the end of 'Splittie' production, but were continued in a different and less elegant style with the Bay-window models. Dual-tone Bays had their body colours complemented by an unexciting white roof panel.

From 1963, Buses came with the option of an extra pair of side-opening doors on the same side as the driver, in addition to the pair on the opposite side. Very few customers availed themselves of this on the grounds of cost. This 21-window Samba remained as luxuriously appointed at the end of production as it was at the beginning, but features like the interior door handles were considered to be of dangerous design by the mid-1960s. The Bay-window was an altogether safer model!

Devons were among the most popular Campers in Britain during the 1960s and 1970s. Well equipped and thoughtfully laid out, they also represented exceptional value for money. By 1965 most retailed at between £400 and £500 more than a de luxe Beetle (£620 in Britain), while the official Westfalias – the most popular conversions in North America – always cost a little more.

Campers were invariably supplied with a 'pop-up' roof that neatly retracted when the vehicle was in use on the road. A quiet spot like this in the English countryside is what Volkswagen camping is all about and remains as popular today as it is was in  the 1950s.

Such is the appeal of the 'Splittie' that these vehicles were adopted by the Peace Movement that emerged in California, and spread worldwide, from the mid-1960s onwards. Today, these vehicles are popularly customised, owners applying their own individual paint schemes and modifications. This example has a pair of 'home-made' rear wheel spats similar to those which were once popular on Beetles.

The Transporter's most useful modification from August 1966 was its 12-volt electrical system. Hitherto, all vehicles had a 6-volt system, except those supplied from 1963 to special order with 12 volts. This change was much appreciated as it minimised the possibility of 'voltage drop' on cold mornings, an important consideration with Camper versions, but the Beetle had to contend with 6-volt electrics for a further twelve months.

After the production of 1.8 million Split-screen Transporters, this model was finally discontinued in 1967 to make way for a much more modern vehicle. Today the Split-screen model is seen in a different light; nostalgia has played a huge part in ensuring that many examples, even the more mundane Pick-ups and Panelvans, have been restored to either original condition or to suit personal taste. It is encouraging that many younger people, born long after the demise of 'Splitties', also appreciate these unique vehicles.

# BAY-WINDOW BUSES, 1967–79

*Launched in August 1967, the second-generation Transporter had a large, one-piece windscreen – hence the name Bay-window – and was much larger and more modern in every way. Early Bays had indicators below the headlamps, domed hubcaps – the Beetle's were of the flat variety from August 1965 – and a step up into the cab on the 'flattened' ends of the front bumper. Do not be fooled by the radial style tread on the tyre casings; these are crossplies and were every bit as undesirable on Bays as they had been on 'Splitties'. For restorers today, this is one piece of originality that is worth sacrificing; crossply tyres as fitted to Volkswagens are, and always have been, a menace.*

# INTRODUCTION

At the time of the Bay's launch in August 1967 there was mayhem on the world's political stage. War between Arabs and Israelis in the Middle East, continuing conflict in Vietnam that outraged large numbers of ordinary American citizens and discord in so many other parts of the world had led to change in the nature of youth culture. Off the coast of Britain a supertanker, the *Torrey Canyon*, caused a huge oil slick – the first of many – raising fears about pollution of the environment. The word 'environment' began to be used in a new way in the English vocabulary.

Ralph Nader and his supporters were busy criticising motor manufacturers over safety issues. A new type of social history was being created by both the Peace Movement, which led to Hippies and 'flower-power', and the pop industry. The Rolling Stones and 'Fab Four' from Liverpool, and a new drug culture initiated by middle-class intellectuals was changing the way in which a whole generation behaved. The Bay-window Bus and Beetle were very much an integral part of this wave of change and not only reflected the new age but helped to shape it.

The Bay-window Bus itself was longer and wider than the 'Splittie', and had a larger, curved, panoramic, one-piece windscreen, which gave the vehicle its popular nickname. It was to a new design with a fresh approach. Although so obviously a Volkswagen, it was very different from the model it replaced, and few of its parts were interchangeable with the old model. Only the domed hubcaps and tail-lamps remained unaltered.

Aesthetically, Bays did not have the 'Splittie's' endearing character or good looks, although many enthusiasts disagreed strongly with this. On the positive side, there was a sliding door on the opposite side to the driver, a much more spacious cabin, fail-safe dual-circuit brakes, maintenance-free ball-joints instead of king and link pin steering, a modern dashboard with a non-reflective upper surface, a more powerful engine in the tail – still air-cooled, naturally – and a top speed in the region of 70mph.

In addition, there were stronger front and rear bumpers, an increasingly important consideration with the huge rise in the volume of traffic by this time. The new Bus also had superior roadholding and handling qualities. Reduction gearboxes in the rear hubs were discontinued and the rear suspension was completely revised along the same lines as the semi-automatic Beetle and Type 4 saloon, both of which were launched in 1968.

Much narrower driveshafts incorporated universal joints on their ends, which allowed the rear wheels to remain upright under hard cornering, rather than adopting the much feared wheel 'tuck-in' that was potentially possible with the 'Splittie's' pure swing-axle system. Transverse torsion-bar suspension with parallel trailing arms continued at both front and rear, although in a 'softened' form, primarily for the benefit of the American market, where soft springing had become the norm.

The *World Car Guide* considered the new Bus to be 'in a class by itself'. This journal's 1970 report commented: 'It's such a practical shape for carrying people and their recreational accoutrement that unfortunately, the tendency is to cram more into it than its engine will handle,' and added; 'The purchase is also an excellent investment. Well-used VW Buses are threatening Detroit's traditional concept of the youth market. Again, escape via a Bus is far less expensive and more promising in terms of birds and bees than being encumbered with a bucket-seated, thirsty-engined GTO or Scat-pack Dodge.'

By 1967, Volkswagen had expanded to the point where there were sufficient resources to release the entire range of Buses at the same time. There was a Panelvan that continued as the best seller, Single- and Double-cab Pick-ups, Kombi, Microbus and Microbus de luxe and High-roof Panelvan. In addition, there were specially equipped ambulances, fire appliances and vehicles for the German armed forces and other public utilities.

The High-roof Panelvan was particularly interesting because the entire roof panel was constructed of fibreglass, a relatively new material in the car industry and not one that was widely used in mass production. Light in weight and never prone to corrosion, this was a brave and pioneering move and one which camper conversion specialists would follow in the 1980s.

The top-of-the-range Microbus de luxe was not as outwardly distinguishable from the 'lesser' models as the 'Splittie' Samba had been, but it was well appointed and provided luxury transport for an increasing number of devotees. For the first twelve months or so of production this model was dubbed 'Clipper', but the name was dropped after a brief legal wrangle with BOAC, the British aeroplane company that was running a Clipper service to and from North America at this time.

On reflection, and this is only with the wisdom of hindsight, one of the reasons why so many people criticised the look of the Bays was possibly less to do with their shape and more to do with the rather dull colours in which these vehicles were painted. The various shades appeared to become fashionably more dreary as the years went by and even the all-white versions had something of a 'skimmed-milk' look about them.

However, Volkswagen's customers did not seem to be concerned with colour schemes. In every way the vehicle was superior to the 'Splittie', from both a passenger's and driver's viewpoint. The high driving position gave a good view over the tops of the hedgerows and oversteer was less likely with the revised rear suspension system. The steering, brake and clutch pedals were light and precise in operation and the vehicles, including utility Pick-ups, drove as well, if not better, than contemporary saloon cars.

The Bay was a marvel and journalists confirmed this time and again. Their road tests revealed a liking for virtually every facet of its design, except its susceptibility to 'wander' in crosswinds due to the rear weight bias. This was an old problem that would never go away while the engine and transaxle remained in the tail, but journalists who did not learn the correct way of dealing with this characteristic were always more proficient in their criticism than they were behind the wheel.

Camper versions became more diverse and almost infinitely more expensive, each converter holding different views about the best way of designing a 'pop-up' roof.

Dutch-built Kemperink Bays, some of which had six wheels and were up to 4 ft longer than the standard vehicles, became much sought after as Campers, even though the majority of conversions were intended for tradespeople such as butchers and bakers.

In 1968, Heinz Nordhoff, the man who had done such a magnificent job of steering Volkswagen into 'big-time' manufacturing, died. One of Wolfsburg's longest public roads, which runs alongside the factory, was named after him in honour of his huge achievements. In August of the same year the Type 4 saloon, the second vehicle intended to be a replacement for the Beetle, was launched, but proved no more successful than the Type 3 saloon had been. Those in charge of the company's saloon division pushed ineffectually for a new type of modern car, but the staff across in Hanover were content in the knowledge that they had performed a good job with the Transporter project. It appeared that they could not put a foot wrong.

Journalists in America and in Germany heaped embarrassing quantities of praise on the Bay and British commentators, particularly Bob Wyse, editor of Volkswagen specialist magazine *Safer Motoring*, considered it to be in a class of its own. So Volkswagen sat back quietly – and perhaps complacently – and made only the usual year-on-year production changes. In 1968 the dashboard switchgear gained identification symbols and, although unnecessary, this at least gave Volkswagen's brochure writers something to be triumphant about.

A collapsible steering column and a cab floor designed to crumple and absorb shock more efficiently in the event of a collision were added next. This was wholly in keeping with contemporary thinking, but was not fully developed until the mid-1970s and later.

By 1970, criticism of the Beetle in the international press had almost reached an all-time high, although sales continued to increase, partially as a result of the Porsche 917's success on the world's racing circuits. To an extent the vitriol also damaged the image of the Bus. Apparently, the 1600 engine was grossly underpowered and in urgent need of replacement.

Criticism of the Bus in this respect, though, was largely aimed at Campers and people carriers. Few journalists in this era ever bothered testing Panelvans and Pick-ups. It had escaped their attention that the 1600cc engine was more than adequate for an average bricklayer, carpenter or plasterer who, at the end of a hard day's labour, rarely had enthusiasm for driving at speeds that journalists considered acceptable for a commercial. Apart from this, a large number of builders usually had a cement mixer perched most precariously on the bed of their trucks, so a high-speed drive to work and back was always out of the question.

In August 1970, the Bus's 1600 engine was endowed with twin-port cylinder heads to assist top-end 'breathing', which also increased engine output from 47bhp to 50bhp. Disc brakes were fitted at the front (drums continued at the rear) four years after the 1500 Beetle was similarly equipped. At the same time, the Bus's road wheels were painted silver (they had been white previously), had circular vents and were fitted with the same style flat hubcaps that had been introduced with the 1300 Beetle in August 1965.

Why twin carburettors were not fitted at this stage is still not clear. The Type 4 saloon had a brace of Solexes from 1968, which improved performance considerably, and the Bus, a much heavier vehicle, demanded more power. To continue with the asthmatic single Solex was almost indefensible, particularly as independent tuning specialists, such as Okrasa in Germany, had been providing power-enhancing engine kits including twin carburettors since the early 1950s. The Okrasa engines were reliable, too, so any argument Volkswagen might have proffered on this matter just did not stand up.

Of Volkswagen's reluctance to improve engine performance, American magazine *Motor Trend* commented

> Despite the addition of disc brakes and a miniscule power increase in the '71 van, VW still persist with their 96cu in engine – less than one third of the size of engines available in any of the Detroit designed vans we drove. So while the '71 minibus radiates the glories-of-a-smaller-outside, nearly-as-big-inside accommodation, more manoeuvrability, better brakes, far superior control, no rattles, easier steering, greater gas mileage, lower upkeep, higher re-sale and rock-bottom investment, the thing still needs more performance.

This sentiment almost precisely echoed most people's attitude towards the Bus by this time. Only a minority applauded the continued use of a low-powered engine. By 1970, exhaust pollution had become a serious issue, especially in California, where smog from harmful emissions blanketed this state's cities. All vehicles built in America, and cars imported into this country had, by this stage been fitted with equipment that attempted to keep emissions to a minimum. The bigger the engine, the worse its pollution; small engines like Volkswagen's were relatively 'clean' and those who cared for the environment and human health considered the German giant's decision to 'think small' a worthy one.

In August 1971, Volkswagen made a compromise between demands for more power and environmental considerations. The Type 4's 1,679cc twin-carburettor engine was slotted into the tail. Developing 66bhp at 4,800rpm, top speed rose to 76mph and in acceleration tests the Bus consistently proved itself capable of reaching the benchmark 60mph from standstill in an acceptable 23 seconds. For a vehicle with the aerodynamic properties of a Norman church tower, this was not a dramatic rise in power but owners appreciated the gain all the same.

Pick-ups were not fitted with the more powerful engine and simply continued with the regular power unit. Following Type 3 and 4 practice, the 1,679cc engine was to the 'suitcase' configuration, with the cooling fan mounted on the rear of the crankshaft. It was a most compact unit as the ancillaries were moved to the sides and rear of the engine and this allowed for the height of the floor above to be lowered to give more luggage space in the rear. Access for servicing was provided by a removable hatch in the floor of the luggage compartment.

This power unit, although not generally as long-lasting as the 1500, gave extremely good service. Its extra power was particularly welcomed by Beetle owners, many of whom cannibalised Buses and Type 4s for their engines which, once installed in a Beetle, gave the latter a reasonable turn of performance.

In this same year all Buses, except Pick-ups, were vastly improved in most markets by having radial tyres fitted as standard. These were long overdue and improved road-holding out of all recognition. Journalists who complained that these 'new-fangled' devices were responsible for an increase in road noise, did this honourable profession no favours.

In August 1972, a revised Bus had square front indicators positioned to the left and right of the fresh-air louvres on the nose panel, instead of below the headlamps as previously, the VW roundel at the front was reduced in size, and a three-speed automatic gearbox was offered, except on Pick-ups, as an extra-cost option. Automatics were obviously more popular in America; this vast population had been fed a large diet of them for decades but enthusiasts remained committed to the normal manuals.

In the following year a 1.8-litre engine was available and had more torque but, developing just 68bhp, was only marginally more powerful than the outgoing 1,679cc unit. The biggest advantage of this new enlarged engine was that it made overtaking easier and safer. Bosch fuel injection replaced carburettors on this model for the American market and it ran more smoothly and economically as a result.

However, none of this could really disguise the fact that the Bay had been in production for a long time. The overall design was sound and never in dispute but, despite the introduction of the 70bhp, 2-litre engine in August 1975, critics continued to demand more performance. The 1973 Middle East oil crisis had hit some sectors of the European motor industry hard and seventeen years after Suez fuel rationing was introduced once again. The result was that  manufacturers produced more fuel-efficient engines, but Volkswagen's air-cooled units still did not create enough power.

The 2 litre was the largest of the company's production flat-fours and, although capable of pushing the Bus along at speeds in excess of 85mph, used enormous quantities of fuel at such a high velocity. Apart from installing improved Girling brakes in 1975, development of the Bay was all but over by the mid-1970s. Like the Beetle, sales gradually tailed away, although Campers were as popular as ever.

Five four-wheel-drive prototypes were constructed in 1978, but there was never a Bay-window production version. Had one come into being, it would have pre-empted this lucrative market long before the Japanese capitalised on it. Internal squabbles between Porsche and Volkswagen – Ferry Porsche greatly favoured four-wheel drive – prevented one and Volkswagen missed out. Many argued that four-wheel drive was unnecessary. They were right, but this did not prevent the industry surging ahead in the 1980s and 1990s with all-wheel drive, a 'craze' that does not appear to be subsiding.

By July 1979, the Bay-window was dead, at least as far as German production was concerned. A special, metallic silver range-topping Microbus with smart velour seats was launched to honour the passing of this second generation Bus, and all were snapped up quickly. In August 1979, the completely fresh third generation Transporter was launched and brought the commercials and people carriers almost, but not quite, totally up to date.

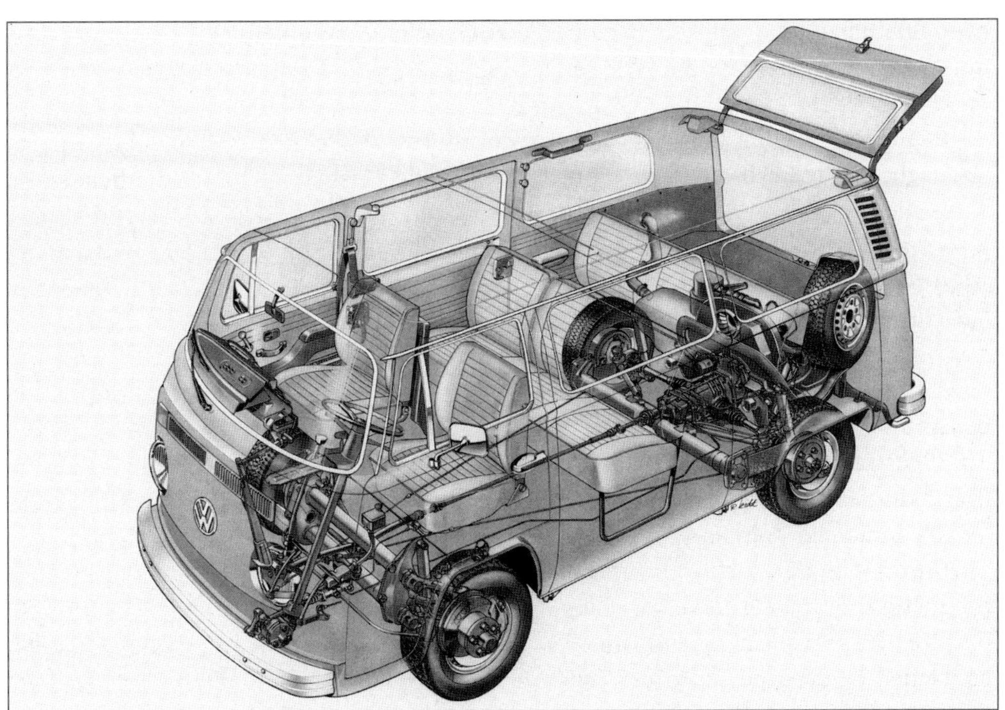

A 'cut-away' drawing that shows just how little the 'box on wheels' actually changed in layout. Transverse torsion-bar suspension continued front and rear but, from the beginning of production, there was a more powerful 1600cc single-port engine in the tail, dual-circuit brakes for added safety, 12-volt electrics and revised driveshafts to give 'fully' independent rear suspension.

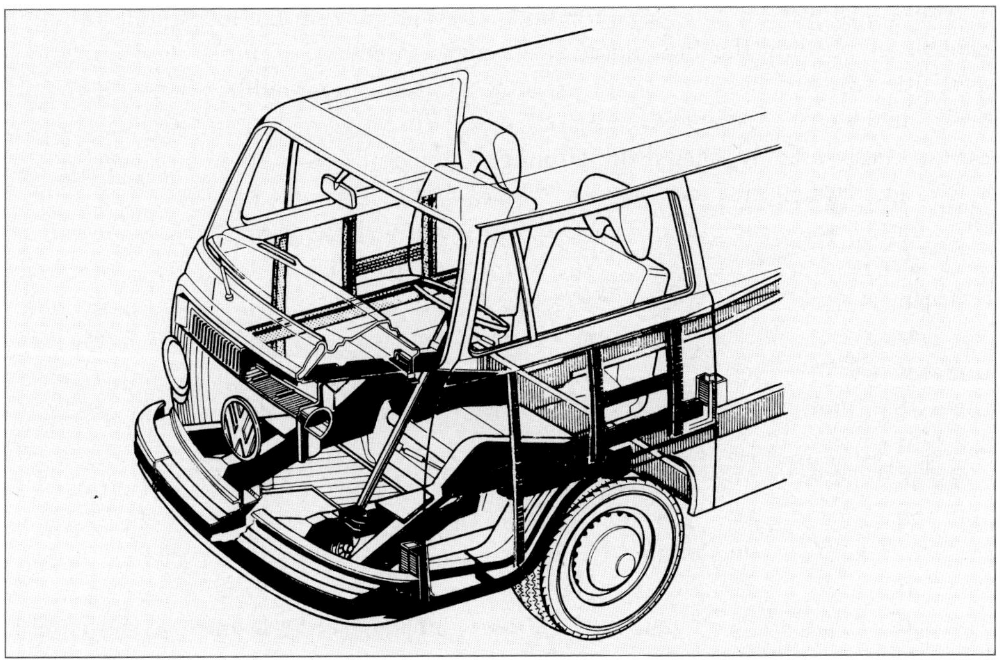

Although of unitary construction, the Transporter utilised two exceptionally strong longitudinal box-section chassis members, which ran the entire length of the vehicle. These were strengthened with crossmembers in 'Splittie' fashion with the floor panels welded integrally. This illustration also shows the revised cabin ventilation system, which draws air from outside through the louvred grille on the front panel.

A Bay's rolling chassis is sturdy and unbreakable, but vulnerable to corrosion. Few rust-inhibiting measures were introduced on these vehicles, which is why so many early examples have needed extensive restoration work. This version from the early 1970s has a twin-carburettor engine, but the suspension system was to the same design laid down by Porsche as early as 1931.

Unlike the 'Splittie' range which was introduced model by model over a long period, the Bay range was complete from the beginning of production. The huge sliding door was a new feature and gave excellent access to the rear load area. The stark Panelvan was arguably the most useful all-rounder and continued as the staple of the Transporter range.

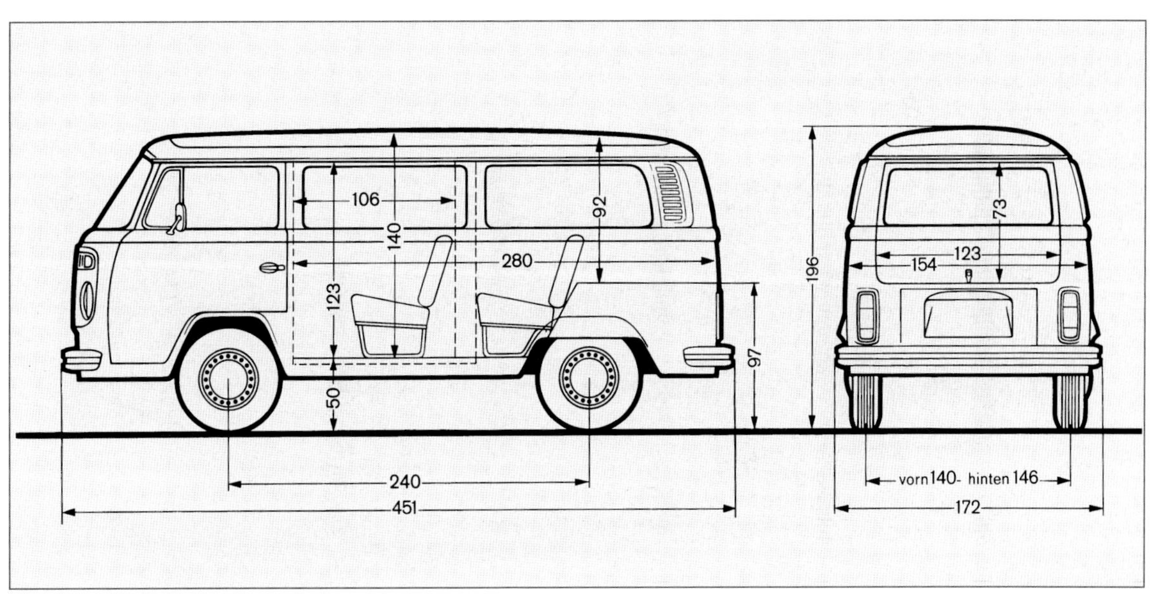

With such a vast expanse of sheet steel bodywork, commercial operators were able to employ the signwriter's art to the full. For this reason the most popularly ordered colour for Panelvans was white.



People-carrying Kombis and Microbuses had longer, elongated windows in place of the 'Splittie's' smaller more square ones. This larger glass area gave the interior a much brighter ambience and added to the feeling of space. Both Kombis and Microbuses were available as 7-, 8- and 9-seaters, although up to 12 people could be accommodated if necessary.

Plain and simple, the Single-cab Pick-up continued to be popular with the building trade on both sides of the Atlantic. These vehicles were commonly overloaded during 'Splittie' days and piled high with sand, tools and all manner of materials. The new 1600 engine enabled builders to transport their loads at a slightly higher speed, which was particularly appreciated on the way home from work.

The Single-cab Pick-up truck was available alternatively with a wooden bed. In reality comparatively few were sold outside the home market and there are few survivors today.

Originally introduced in the late 1950s, the wide-bodied Pick-up was made in response to demands from the building trade. A Westfalia conversion, this model allowed heavier, larger loads to be carried.

The Pick-up's side flaps and tailgate are bottom-hinged, simply latched and could be folded down for loading purposes in a matter of seconds. By today's standards the load platform would be considered too high, but rarely presented problems for the muscle-bound men of previous years.

The fabulous Double-cab Pick-up, originally debuted in 1958, was, in many ways, a more useful vehicle than its Single-cab sister, despite its lack of a locker-bed below the main load platform. Although intended purely for utility purposes, these make for ideal family transport – up to six adults can be accommodated in the spacious cab – and are much sought after today, particularly by younger enthusiasts. Note the style of the typically Germanic ventilation louvres in the cab's 'C' posts.

The Double-cab's single rear door was always on the opposite side to the driver, the truck assuming something of a slab-sided appearance on this side. Nothing spoiled the Transporter's appearance, however, more than than the massive bumper overriders, which were compulsory in some markets by the 1970s.

Both Single- and Double-cab Pick-ups came with the option of fitting bows and a tarpaulin above the rear load area. As these cost extra, they were not particularly popular in Britain, where tradespeople had long since adapted to the appalling weather, without having to resort to using such items as canvas tarpaulins.

The High-roof Panelvan – rare in Britain – was unusual in that it was among the first mass-produced vehicles to utilise fibreglass; the roof was entirely made of this material. Favoured by the German post office and clothing trade, these made for superb and relatively quick delivery vehicles. The vast majority led exceptionally hard lives, being hammered on the German autobahn network for the greater part of their lives. Survivors in good condition are very uncommon.

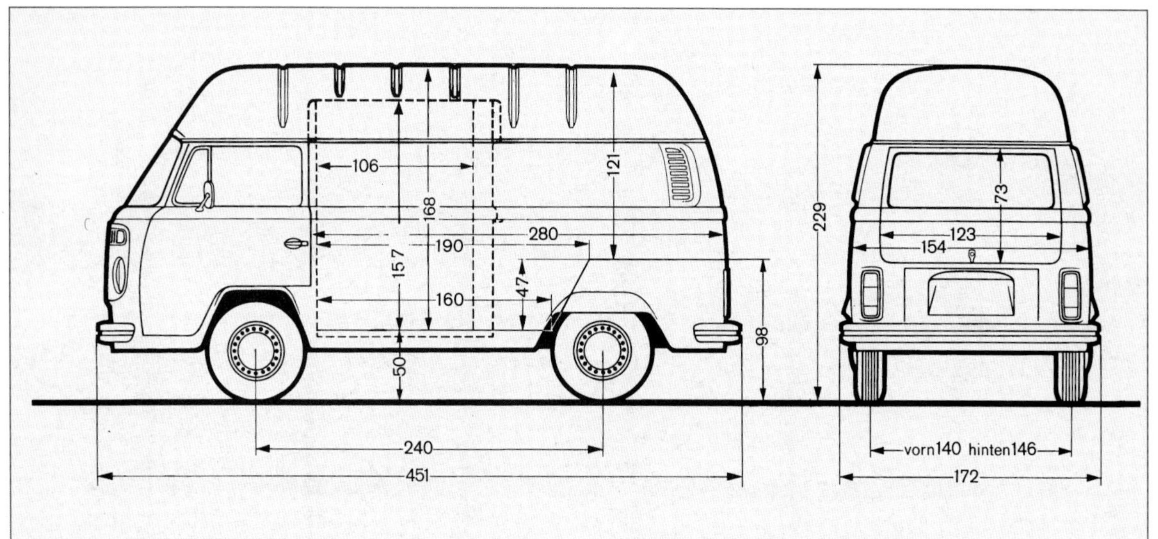

High-roof Panelvans were substantially taller than the regular models, and also had a revised sliding side door. Fully laden, the original 1600 engine struggled to pull these vehicles along at much above 55mph, but few ever failed to reach their destination.

The Bay-window Kombi, with its painted bumpers and relative lack of bodywork bright trim, was the cheapest and most popular of the people carriers. Many American journalists were so impressed with these vehicles that they wondered why anyone bothered to drive a conventional saloon. Their point was well received but their question had been answered by the mid-1970s; good as these vehicles were, their engines used too much fuel and were underpowered.

The range-topping Microbus, originally dubbed 'Clipper', was improved – some think overburdened – by an alloy 'waistline' moulding during the 1970s. This matched similar treatment applied to the range-topping 'Splittie' Samba but looked incongruous on the more modern vehicle. Lamborghini are to be applauded for their pioneering moves to dispense with bright trim on the Miura in 1967, but here was Volkswagen adding quantities of it in 1973.

In contrast to the 'Splittie's' simple painted metal dashboard with a single instrument, the Bay's was very modern. There was a full complement of gauges and the dashboard itself was in more fashionable, non-reflecting black plastic. Unlike the 'Splittie's' stylish steering wheel, the Bay's plain black item was utterly devoid of character, famously on the large side but extremely comfortable to use.

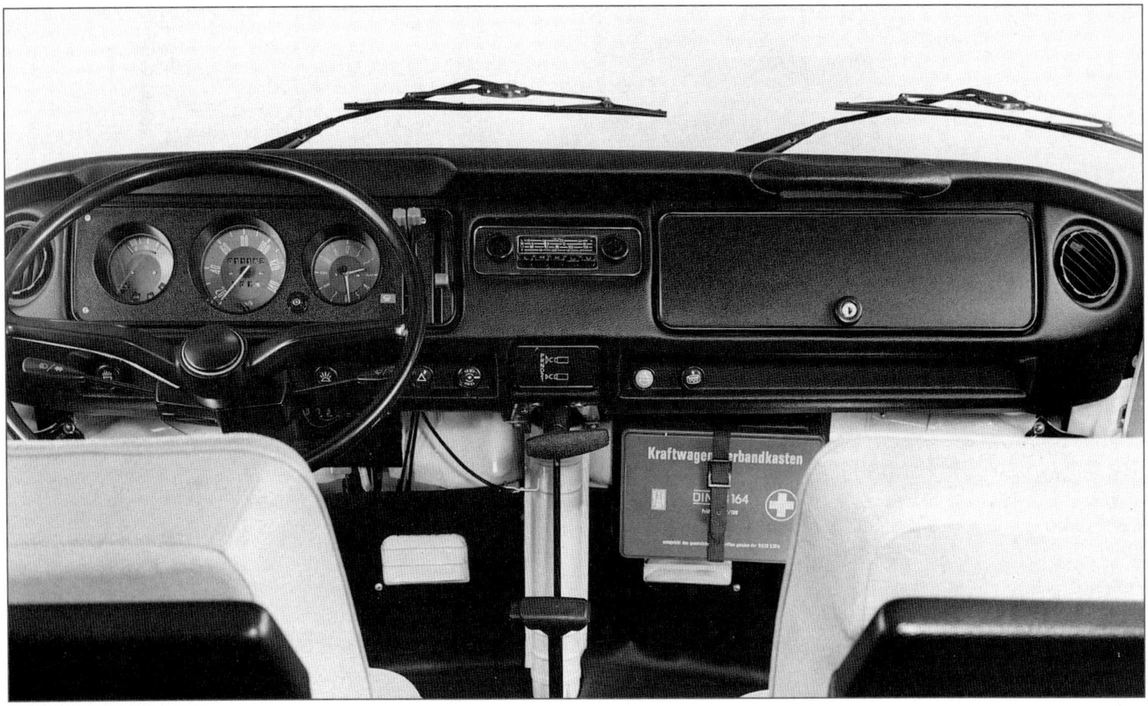

In addition to more modern instrumentation there was a modern, lockable glovebox (though not on all models), switchgear in soft, black plastic with identification symbols, swivelling fresh-air vents on the extreme right and left of the dashboard and a passenger's grab handle in 'easy-grip' soft plastic. A first-aid kit was a useful addition but was not supplied as standard fitment.

The Bay's revised fresh-air ventilation system collected air from the vertical louvres in the front panel and directed it through large-diameter conduits attached to the cab doors. Airflow was manually controlled by buttons on the rear outlets. For the benefit of passengers in the back, it was a huge improvement over the 'Splittie's' metal distribution box on the underside of the cab roof.

Modern door locks first appeared on Bays and replaced the 'Splittie's' locking door handles situated on the interior door panels. The items seen here, incidentally, have a nasty habit of becoming unscrewed and falling on to the floor, never to be found again.

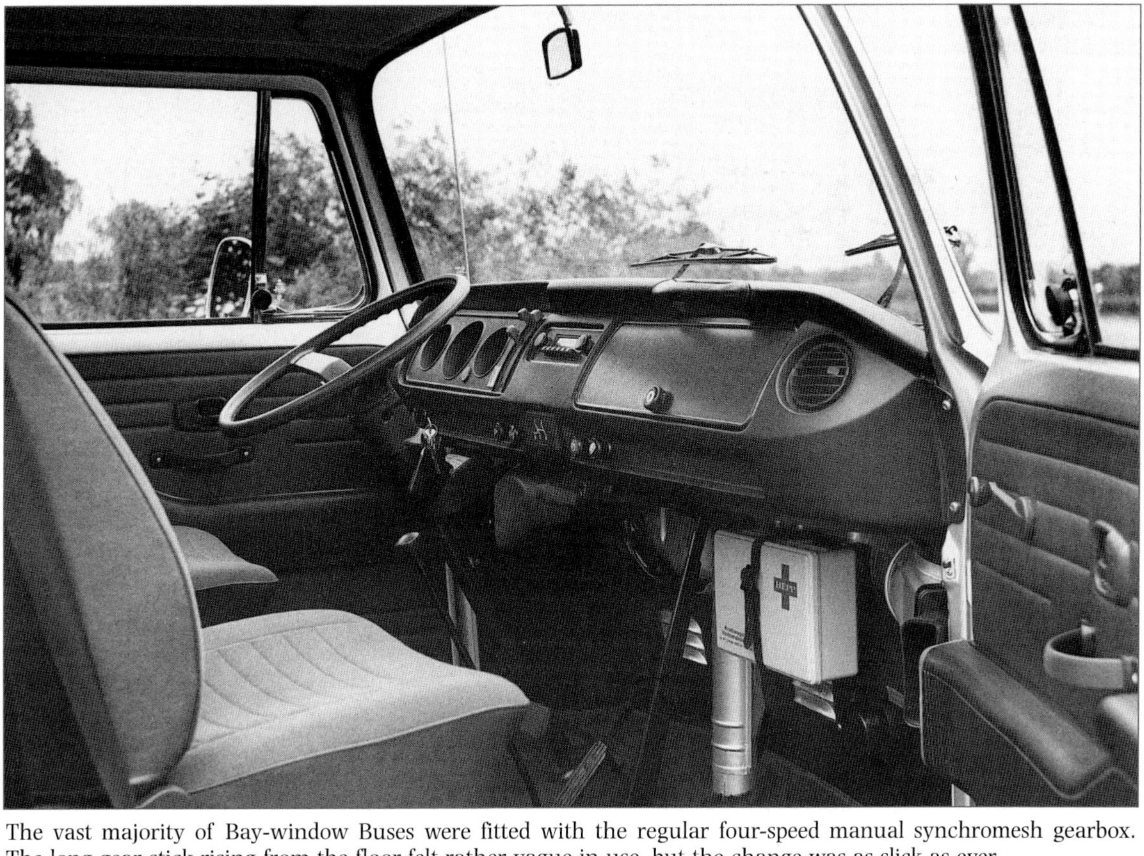

The vast majority of Bay-window Buses were fitted with the regular four-speed manual synchromesh gearbox. The long gear stick rising from the floor felt rather vague in use, but the change was as slick as ever.

With the seats and rubber mats removed the structure of the Kombi is shown to good effect. The floor panels are corrugated for extra strength and the roof bows give the structure immense torsional rigidity. For the purpose of fitting an elevating roof, most Camper converters were

compelled to remove the central bow, which is just one of the reasons why Volkswagen never became involved in this specialist market.

A higher standard of trim, including a full headlining, vinyl side panelling (with horizontal alloy mouldings) and high-quality upholstery, was the hallmark of the de luxe Microbus. The sunroof is a steel sliding item, standard on this model, unless specifically ordered without one. Grab handles attached to the roof suffice for passenger safety, although seat belts were fitted from the mid-1970s onwards.

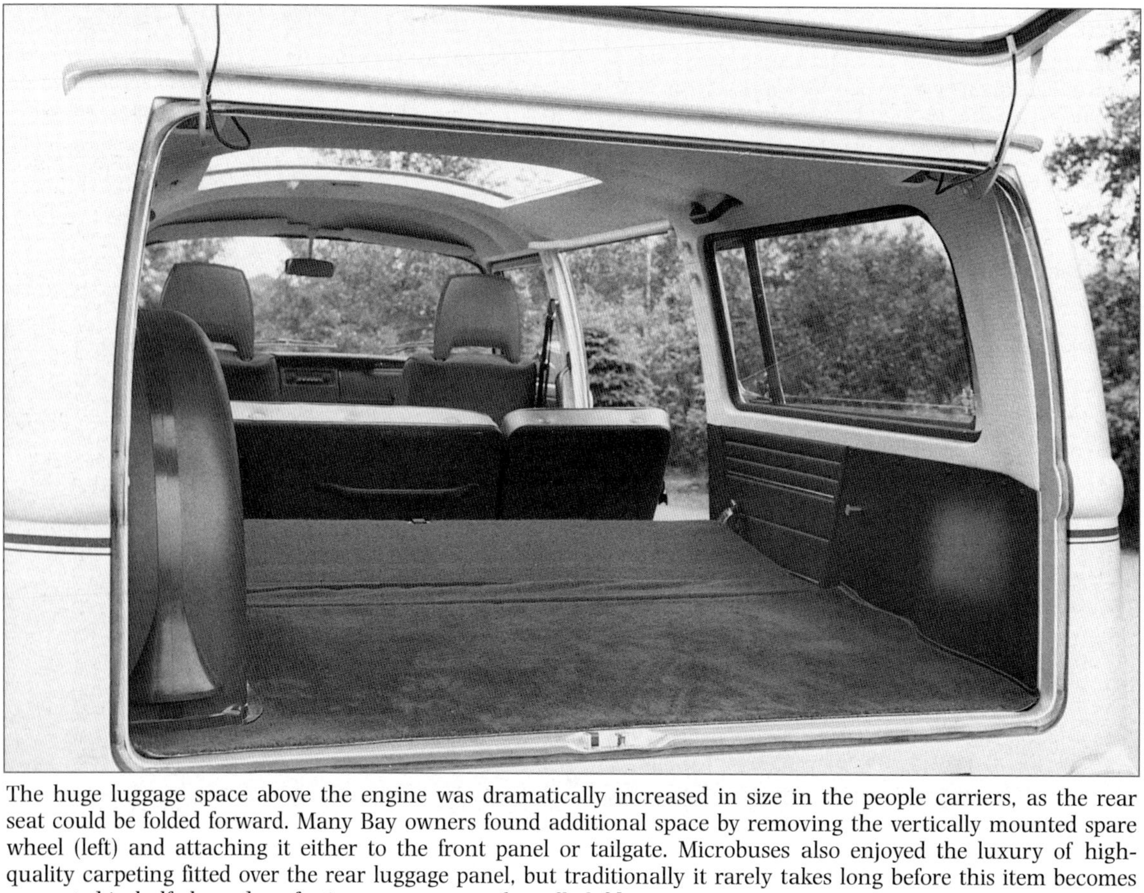

The huge luggage space above the engine was dramatically increased in size in the people carriers, as the rear seat could be folded forward. Many Bay owners found additional space by removing the vertically mounted spare wheel (left) and attaching it either to the front panel or tailgate. Microbuses also enjoyed the luxury of high-quality carpeting fitted over the rear luggage panel, but traditionally it rarely takes long before this item becomes encrusted in half-chewed confectionery courtesy of small children!

Clean, plain styling – the Bay had style, if not the 'Splittie's' 'old world' character. These vehicles are still plentiful and understandably form the backbone of the enthusiasts' movement today. In the twenty-first century it is not inconceivable that there will be modern 'retro-clones' of both 'Splitties' and Bays. Classic designs just never age!

Bay-window Campers were invariably fitted with elevating roofs, which in many cases were made of fibreglass and folded neatly away. The roof of the Westfalia seen here was of this type. Such retractable roofs did not interfere with or upset the vehicle's aerodynamics.

Idyllic mountain scenes were carefully chosen by Volkswagen's public relations people to advertise the benefits of Campers. This Westfalia, with a rear-hinged elevating roof and integral reversing lights, dates from the mid-1970s when Bays were just about at the height of their popularity. Note that an electrical socket is located on the side of the bodywork below the rear side windows.

Great rivals side by side, the Volkswagen Microbus is dwarfed by the overtaking Mercedes-Benz Panelvan. The Stuttgart concern would also manufacture a similar vehicle to Volkswagen's Transporter; it was exceptionally well made and every bit as reliable but never as popular as the original concept from Wolfsburg.

Such was the quality of Westfalia's fixtures and fittings, that the majority survived the attentions of children over the years, and there are many such vehicles still in existence to prove it. The wood veneer, incidentally, featured in several camping conversions during the 1970s and was generally very expensive, but would not meet with today's simpler standards of design.

Early Bay Westfalia Campers had an elevating roof hinged at the front. Well-appointed Westfalias,
like so many other conversions, had a central dining table (easily folded away), ample wardrobe

space, a sink close to the sliding door and a gas-fired cooker.

A Bay-window test 'mule', not just being put through its paces, but tested ultimately to destruction, 1970s. Many motoring enthusiasts consider the job of official test driver to be the finest form of employment anyone could wish for. In reality, it is laborious, potentially dangerous, extremely time consuming and carries a great deal of responsibility. Unusually, this mid-1970s Bay has domed hubcaps, which were replaced by flat items on production vehicles from 1970.

Another test vehicle demonstrates its climbing ability on rough, slippery ground, for which the exhaust pipe has been raised and rerouted through a 'cut-out' in the rear bumper. Test vehicles always led exceptionally hard lives. This one shows clear signs of a hectic test schedule: spilt fuel has left two nasty stains on the bodywork below the filler cap.

With its engine and gearbox in the rear, the Transporter's traction made these vehicles particularly popular in rural areas all over the world and as expedition vehicles. Four-wheel drive was not strictly necessary in most applications but this did not stop Volkswagen from developing one during 1978.

A Volkswagen publicity picture in which the photographer has waited for the Bus to make a little splash in a puddle of water – it is not clear what this proves as all vehicles splash water when driven through puddles. The real point is that the Transporter, with its tough torsion-bar suspension, was equally happy being driven hard down a road like this as it was on a smooth motorway.

During the mid-1960s the VW Bus and Beetle were adopted as symbols by the middle-class Peace Movement, which existed primarily to protest about the USA's conflict with Communists in Vietnam. The 'alternative' clothing adopted by this movement that led to the 'Flower Power' people is merely hinted at by this girl's headdress. This was a little sign of acknowledgement on Volkswagen's part of contemporary fashion.

Another wonderful publicity shot of 'happy girl at wheel of Microbus'. Official photographers were greatly relieved that the flat hubcaps introduced in 1970 did not allow them to be reflected in the chrome, as they often had been with the previous domed items. But, there they are, captured for posterity in the front bumper instead!

There were as many special bodies built for Bays as 'Splitties'. This is the Dutch-made Kemperink Bay which, being some 4 ft longer than the standard Panelvan, proved to be popular with butchers and bakers. This particular example has been converted into a Camper in recent times and has a vast amount of interior space.

The Kemperink's interior can sleep up to four in comfort and six at a push. This example is fully kitted out with every conceivable extra, including a shower, cooking facilities, toilet, wardrobes, dining table and seating. It makes for an ideal continental touring machine.

Campers came with a variety of 'pop-up' roof designs. This rectangular version with vinyl side skirts allowed for a reasonable amount of headroom but provided cramped sleeping conditions, except for small children.

The Martin Walter side-elevating roof was arguably the best all-round compromise in extending roofs. Headroom was good, even for the tallest people, and it could be fitted with a bunk bed on either side. Condensation on the inside of the vinyl skirt could present problems in certain weather conditions, however. The British-based Martin Walter company also manufactured the famous Dormobile Camper conversion.

Fixed roofs made of fibreglass were popular from the 1980s and many Bays had these fitted 'retrospectively'. Although their height means that these vehicles cannot be parked in an average garage, they have the advantage of being safely and permanently erected and aerodynamically shaped for good handling characteristics in crosswinds.

Several Camper conversions had their spare wheels mounted on the nose panel to create additional space inside the vehicle. This concealed the VW roundel but Volkswagen did not seem to mind. Anyone who could not recognise a VW Transporter by the 1970s had probably lived a sheltered existence.

Special bodies were not just the preserve of independent Camper converters. Volkswagen produced several variations on the Transporter theme, this Pick-up being one that was also popular in the building trade. The tipper-bed is hydraulically operated on a single ram.

With its fibreglass roof bonded to the metal bodywork, the High-roof Panelvan allowed for loads and equipment – some of an unusual nature – to be stacked high. This model proved to be hugely popular among a number of public service utilities and private concerns in Germany. With so much additional interior space, this Transporter was capable of housing large quantities of special equipment for a multitude of applications. Note the fabulous and typically German bridge.

The majority of larger hotels in Germany throughout the 1970s had at least one Panelvan for delivery purposes and general duties. Many had a courtesy Kombi or Microbus as well. That so many thousand survive today is testimony to Volkswagen's continuing commitment to the highest levels of build quality. Incidentally, parked outside Lufthansa's offices across the street is a Renault 16, an innovative hatchback launched in the mid-1960s, but there are virtually no survivors today . . . anywhere.

Follow the leader – test vehicles stream from the factory. Volkswagen have always given journalists and factory test drivers a heavy daily schedule for the purpose of discovering a new vehicle's true potential and flaws. Covering 400 miles per day is not unusual on a 'press launch' but ultimately this is the only way in which a true assessment of the Bay's merits could be made.

A Transporter in the making during the 1970s. The wiring looms are complex and can only be fitted by qualified, experienced auto electricians, which is one reason why restoring one properly today is such an expensive and time-consuming business.

Three-speed automatic transmission Transporters were available from 1972; they were distinguished externally by a badge on the tailgate and 'bumpy' engine note on up and down changes. Auto transmission and utility box was something of a contradiction but the world had changed, largely for the better by this time. These vehicles were especially popular in North America, where automatic transmission had been the norm for many years.

The launch of automatic transmission coincided with the introduction of the 1.7-litre engine, but this was not available on Pick-up trucks. Based on assumptions about the reliability of indigenous motoring products, British Volkswagen enthusiasts generally kept faith with the manual gearbox versions.

The original Bay's door handle fitted to the sliding side door had an integral lock, which was located separately from 1974. Small detail changes like this were typical of so many carried out under the banner of 'development and improvement', but were of little consequence in practical terms.

## 1. Transporter-Generation 1950 bis 1967

Im reichlich dimensionierten Motorraum mit luftgekühlter 1,1-Liter-Vierzylinder-Boxermaschine haben rechts das Reserverad und links der Kraftstofftank Platz.

## 2. Transporter-Generation 1967 bis 1979

Außer der Heckklappe für Wartungs- und Servicearbeiten ist der Motor von oben zur Durchführung von Reparaturarbeiten zugänglich. Zum 1,6-Liter-Boxer- mit stehendem Gebläse kommt 1971 ein 1,7-Liter-Flachmotor (Foto) hinzu. Er wird 1978 im Hubraum auf 2,0-Liter und in der Leistung auf 51 kW (70 PS) angehoben.

## 3. Transporter-Generation ab August 1979

Eine weitere Absenkung des Motorraums wird durch die konstruktive Vereinheitlichung der luftgekühlten Boxer-Motoren mit Kühlluftgebläse auf der Kurbelwelle möglich. Große Klappe über dem Motorraum, tägliche Kontrolle von hinten durch wegklappbare Kennzeichenbefestigung. Der seitlich geneigt eingebaute, wassergekühlte Reihen-Dieselmotor begnügt sich mit dem gleichen Platzangebot wie die luftgekühlten Boxer-Triebwerke.

Three generations of the classic air-cooled flat-four ranging from the original 1,131cc unit up to the most powerful 2-litre 'suitcase' engine. The latter was actually introduced in 1972 in 1.7-litre form and was much more compact than the traditional unit. Hundreds of detail modifications were made to the engine down the years, as is readily apparent here, but the power unit remained fundamentally unchanged. Note the remarkable amount of space around the engine in the top picture.

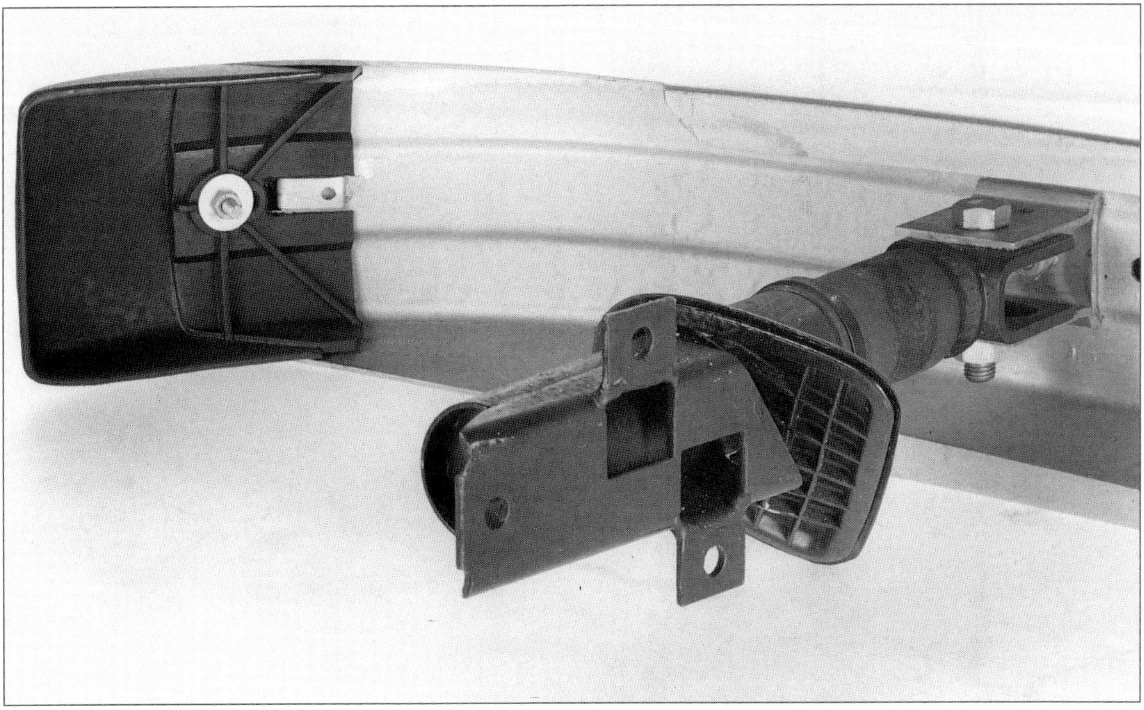

Energy absorbing bumpers were practical safety items but were among the many modified components that brought an increase in weight to the vehicle in the 1970s.

The prototype of the Bay-window Elektromobil was developed in conjunction with the Rhine-Westfalia Electrical Company, and first shown in August 1972. The vehicle had a payload of 800 kg and developed 44bhp, equivalent to the output of the Beetle 1500's conventional engine.

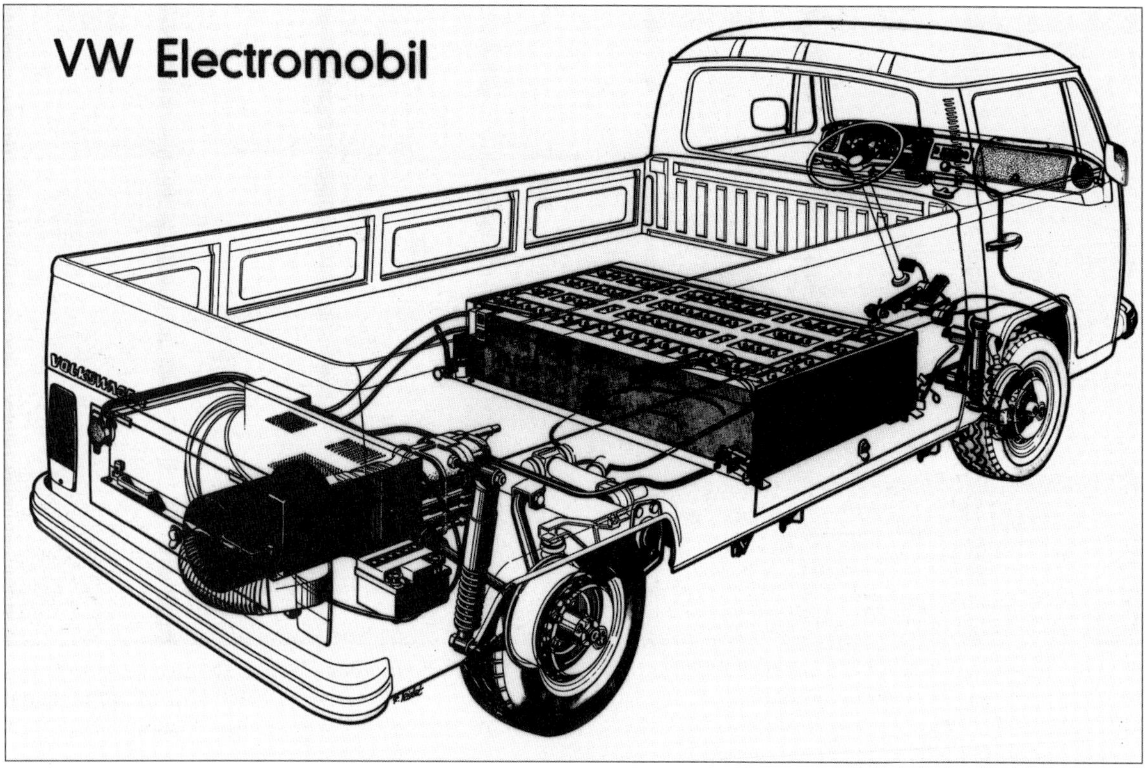

# VW Electromobil

The massive batteries for the Elektromobil vehicles, seen here in Pick-up form, were housed amidships, but the project never got beyond prototype stage. Battery power is one area of research that has failed dismally; alcohol fuels provide a much more practical alternative, as Brazilian engine manufacturers continue to prove year after year.

The prototype Elektromobil's 44bhp electric motor is mated to the standard transaxle in the normal way, but takes up considerably less space than the conventional power unit.

The electric-powered Pick-up truck in full flight; this vehicle was by all accounts pleasant to drive because it was so much quieter than the conventional vehicles. However, whereas petrol-driven Bays had a range of about 300 miles, this device needed its batteries recharging after less than 100 miles, which is the biggest drawback, of course, of battery power.

A four-seater Cushman buggy provides speedy transport for those touring Volkswagen's vast factories. Here, dozens of chromed hubcaps are stacked one on top of the other prior to being fitted. Performed 'in-house', Volkswagen's standard of chromium-plating has never been equalled anywhere in the motor industry.

A rather elaborate, if typically German, way of demonstrating the load-carrying capacity of the Pick-up truck. The locker-bed below the main platform provided useful storage space; members of the building trade, however, traditionally utilised the locker for housing flat shovels – and little else – on which they cooked eggs, bacon and fried bread for lunch.

Without the option of the tarpaulin to cover the load bed, the Pick-up did not make for ideal delivery transport in wet weather. This truck is a 1970 model with vented wheels and flat hubcaps, but the delivery man's sideburns date this photograph a lot later.

More than any other commercial vehicle, the Single-cab Pick-up has arguably contributed as much to the social history of the twentieth century as Coca-Cola, the long-playing record and denim jeans have done. Computers and associated technology will not only contribute to the social history of the twenty-first century, but control it. However, scientists have yet to discover a better way of transporting bricks to a building site than in one of these vehicles.

Like this example, all Pick-ups had to work very hard for a living. Heavy loads, many of which were of a paint damaging, body crushing nature, took their toll and scrapyards reaped rich rewards.

Volkswagen's large LT commercial range of vehicles began production at the Hanover plant from April 1975; they were made alongside the regular Bay-window Transporters. These vehicles – most were Panelvans initially – had much greater carrying capacity and a bigger payload. They were built in response to the changing needs of operators in a more modern commercial world. All LTs had water-cooled engines, which in 2-litre form would eventually power the Porsche 924.

*LT Panelvans await their wheels, roof panels and final finishing on the Hanover assembly lines. These vehicles appear to have been passed over by most Volkswagen enthusiasts but make for spacious and versatile people carriers for those who have sufficient time to carry out the necessary conversion work.*

By October 1982, Volkswagen had celebrated production of the 2-millionth LT Transporter. This was yet another of the company's big volume sellers. Not strictly comparable, but it is interesting nonetheless, that 2 million examples of the Morris Minor were sold between 1948, when production of this so-called Beetle rival began, and 1972 when production finally halted. Little wonder, therefore, that the British motor industry is largely under the control of Germans today.

In the modern age the infamous school run is performed by a multitude of popular MPV vehicles, such as the Renault Espace, and a plethora of gas-guzzling, four-wheel drive 'Tonka Toys', but it all started with the Volkswagen Kombi. By the 1970s, hundreds of education authorities in German-speaking countries used Bays for transporting pupils to and from school for the simple reason that there was nothing better available.

Half a dozen Kombis await passengers destined for a safari holiday in the African bush. The girl's trousers and Transporters' rear lights with integral reversing lights date this scene to the mid-1970s. However, there is a serious 'joker' in the pack – a Mazda pick-up truck sits between two Transporters. Competition from the Japanese by this time posed a serious threat to Volkswagen and other European manufacturers. Twenty years on the Japanese economy would be on the brink of collapse, the German one as strong as ever.

Another VW specifically for use on safari in Africa. By the late 1960s and early 1970s, Transporters were used all over the world for expedition work, despite the availability of four-wheel drives such as the Land Rover. With extra carrying capacity and almost unrivalled traction on slippery terrain, a VW was the obvious choice for thousands. The small circular reflectors below the headlamps were mandatory in some, but by no means all, markets.

Painted in an uninspiring shade of khaki, Bay-window Pick-ups, Panelvans and Kombis were supplied to the German armed forces. Many were equipped with guns and other special equipment.

German police, fire and ambulance services found many uses for the VW Bus. A viable alternative was not available for the most part but by the mid-1970s most were demanding that Volkswagen produce a vehicle with greater power.

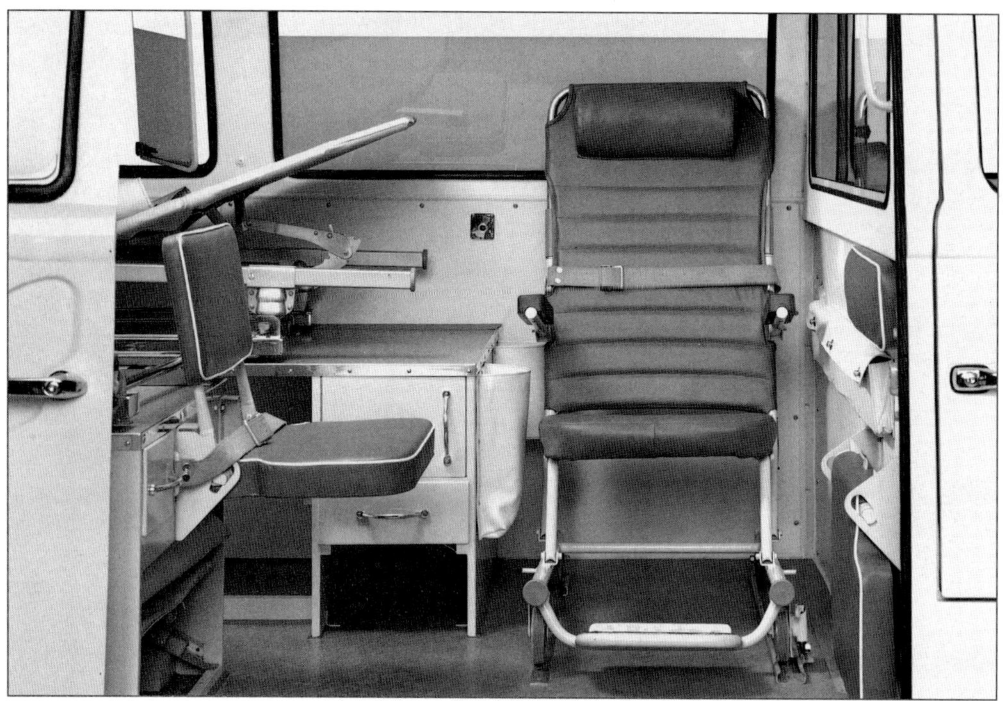

Ambulance versions were officially available from Volkswagen by 1951, although the Bonn-based Miesen concern had supplied a similar vehicle from November of the previous year. The majority were kitted out by German health authorities to suit their own specific needs. This Bay has facilities to accommodate two patients and the same number of qualified medical staff. Volkswagen ambulances have considerable curiosity value today and are much sought after.

The very best of luck to you, sir! Towing a large trailer and boat with even the most powerful 2-litre Bus was never easy, especially with a Camper that was also fully loaded with special equipment. Combined with a relative lack of power, fuel consumption was heavy with a load like this, despite the many optimistic claims made by owners.

This is the only image that appears to exist anywhere of the four-wheel-drive prototype built towards the end of Bay-window production in 1978. One of these vehicles would have been a welcome and lucrative addition to the range – Ferry Porsche was heavily in favour – but internal politics at Volkswagen prevented a production version and the company missed out on an explosive market.

Close to the end of production Volkswagen offered this beautiful top-of-the-range Microbus in metallic silver. Fitted with almost every conceivable 'extra', it was a truly luxurious machine and marked the end of Bay-window production. Note that the rectangular spotlamps are not in keeping with circular headlamps.

The metallic silver Buses of 1978 and 1979 had a steel sliding sunroof and blue velour upholstery as standard, but these vehicles were far from cheap and generally fell into the hands of affluent folk who needed to ferry their children about.

Once aboard and ready to go, this family, in contrast to the usual miseries and tantrums that typify a day out, appear to be happy and smiling.

Long after the demise of the Bay-window in 1979,
Camper versions continued to be popular. Resale
values remained high and a number of independent
converters snapped up secondhand examples for the
purpose of continuing their trade. Curiously, this
trend continues – Bay-window Campers, it appears,
just will not be allowed to die.

As the message on this Dormobile Camper's handbook
makes clear, a Volkswagen is the 'passport to new
frontiers'.

During the 1990s the Bay-window model has proved to be the most popular of Volkswagen's Transporters among customisers. This Camper has been denuded of its external bright trim, has lowered suspension and a set of American-made, EMPI-style, five-spoke, alloy wheels.

While rear-engined, air-cooled Transporter production would continue after 1979 in Europe, German Beetle production was ended permanently in 1978. Ironically, both Bay-windows and Beetles are produced in South America today, the Beetle in Mexico, the Transporter in Brazil.

# CHAPTER FIVE

# WENT THE DAY TO A WEDGE, 1979–82

*The third-generation Wedge Transporter was announced as a successor to the Bay-window in 1979. The air-cooled engine continued to be mounted in the rear in tandem with the gearbox but the vehicle had been substantially revised. The new vehicle was larger, more spacious, had an increased glass area and a frontal shape designed to penetrate air more effectively.*

# INTRODUCTION

Popularly nicknamed the 'Wedge' after its steeply raked frontal aspect, the third-generation Bus was very different from its predecessors. Volkswagen's designers were given a brief for a wholly new vehicle, a bolder, larger beast, and they accomplished this with ease.

Although their efforts resulted in a Bus for the modern age, it bore all the usual hallmarks of a genuine Volkswagen. Build quality was exemplary – quality engineering at it best – but the vehicle also had some of the character that had evolved with the 'Splittie' and disappeared to a certain degree with the Bay.

Not only was the new body bigger and more spacious internally, it was also able to penetrate the air more efficiently. At this stage aerodynamics were beginning to play an increasingly important role in the design of both passenger saloons and sports cars; much of what had been learnt, primarily in Grand Prix and sports car racing, was naturally absorbed by those developing commercial vehicles.

The Wedge's windscreen was huge, even by Bay standards, and more curvaceous to aid smooth airflow over the sides and top of the bodywork. For the time being, the all-important underside was ignored, but Volkswagen had at least made a good start in employing aerodynamic theory.

An enlarged sliding door was positioned on the side of the bodywork, opposite the driver as usual, but 'Splittie' fans – sceptics almost to a man – were excused for laughing at the rear end of the new vehicle. Here there was a massive, top-hinged tailgate! Few could resist the urge to nickname the Wedge as the 'Mk2 Barn-door'. This facet of VW Transporter design had revolved through a full circle and added considerable weight to the idea that Ben Pon's original idea of 1947 was indeed as sound as ever – even in the 1980s.

During 'Splittie' and Bay days the location of the spare wheel had always been awkward, particularly for Camper converters. In standard guise the Bay's spare wheel was placed on the left-hand side of the rear luggage compartment, which inevitably took up space that could have otherwise been usefully occupied by luggage. Several owners and independent camping specialists addressed this inconvenience by bolting the spare wheel to the outside of the bodywork, either at the front or rear. Neither was entirely satisfactory. Attached to the tailgate it was a particular nuisance, as the wheel added weight and made it difficult to open the door, a heavy item in itself. At the front the wheel impaired air-flow to the cabin, upset the vehicle's aerodynamics and increased fuel mileage.

To open up more space inside the vehicle, the spare wheel was finally placed well out of harm's way below the cab floor behind the front bumper. This was a wonderful arrangement – until a puncture occurred. Extracting the spare wheel and tyre, not to mention installing the 'flat', inevitably led to a grubby pair of trousers.

As with the Bay, the entire range was complete upon the vehicle's launch. There was a Panelvan, High-roof Panelvan, Single- and Double-cab Pick-up trucks,

Kombi, Microbus and Microbus de luxe, as well as the usual host of specials kitted out to cater for public utilities, mostly in Germanic countries. Other countries tended to be a little more patriotic when it came to vehicles for public service functions.

In producing the Wedge, Volkswagen had made a deliberate decision to take the range 'up-market', and for good reason. The days of 'penny-pinching', austerity and hardship were well and truly over. Customers demanded much more from motoring manufacturers, and were in a good position to pay for luxury. There was also stronger and increased competition from rival manufacturers.

To this end the Wedge had a modern, revised dashboard with a full complement of instruments, improved quality vinyl or velour upholstery (depending on the model) and better-quality floor coverings. Through-flow ventilation was improved, with more outlet vents in the interior, which were designed in such a way as to be less conspicuous than on previous models.

Although construction of the body/chassis unit was much the same as ever – twin longitudinals with crossmembers and outriggers welded to the floor panels – the suspension was completely revised and many argued that this was very much for the better.

The tough, and almost unbreakable, torsion-bar system that had given such worthy service on 'Splitties' and Bays, not to mention Beetles, Type 3s and Karmann Ghias, was dispensed with altogether. Torsion-bar springing had always been associated with Volkswagen and Porsche – indeed, Porsche had patented this unique system as early as 1931 – and as a suspension medium it was practically unrivalled. It was certainly unusual, but gave excellent ride quality and could be 'tuned' for an almost infinite number of terrain applications. Apart from the front leaves requiring a dab of grease now and again, this was a part of classic Volkswagens that owners did not need to worry about.

However, torsion bars had a couple of major drawbacks; they were relatively expensive to produce and, as they were mounted transversely front and rear, ate into potentially large quantities of luggage space. In their place were coil springs, wishbones and anti-roll bar at the front, and coil springs and trailing arms at the rear. As a bonus there was rack-and-pinion steering for lighter, more precise handling. During this era of development, coil springs and wishbones were virtually *de rigueur* in the motor industry, although the majority of passenger cars had been favoured with MacPherson struts, if not at the rear, more often than not at the front.

Among Volkswagen traditionalists the change to coil springs provoked something of an outcry. Despite this, there was no denying that the change made a general improvement to the Wedge's road manners, if not its road-holding. Some journalists of course commented, as before, about the rear weight bias and the tendency to oversteer.

In reality the new Wedge was never prone to oversteer, unless driven at the kind of ridiculous speeds that would have seen their front-engined counterparts, and even most well-honed sports machinery, disappearing into ditches. Test journalists who wrote about the tail-end of a Wedge breaking away were, I fear, rather given to fanciful imaginations.

There were just two engine options, namely, the traditional 50bhp twin-port 1600 and 70bhp, 2-litre lump. In most European countries, the 2 litre was fitted with twin Solex carburettors, whereas Bosch fuel injection was standard wear on exports to North America. The 1600 had a single Solex as usual.

The 1600 engine was woefully inadequate in coping with the Wedge's additional bulk, and it came as no surprise that this did not escape journalists. This time they really did have a point. On a flat road the 1.6-litre unit was capable of driving the Wedge along at a comfortable, if slightly strained, 65 to 70mph. But, an uphill gradient saw this figure slip appreciably downward and most drivers got fed up with having to change down a 'cog' in an attempt to maintain anything resembling reasonable pace.

It had not slipped the attention of Volkswagen's loyal clientele that their mounts were still only equipped with a four-speed gearbox (or three-speed automatic transmission), and fuel consumption suffered – well below 20mpg in certain circumstances – without the benefit of an 'overdrive' fifth ratio. Many, if not most, contemporary vehicles had five-speed gearboxes as standard – the Wedge did not and this made no sense at all to owners.

From 1975, the company's range of passenger cars, which included the Golf, Passat, Scirocco and Polo, were powered by transversely mounted, water-cooled engines driving the front wheels. The conventional four-cylinder power units, with their cast-iron blocks and overhead camshafts, produced a great deal more power than the air-cooled engines. The latter had been shown to be potentially capable of producing huge quantities of power in racing Porsches and tuned rally and racing Beetles. However, extracting large performance potential from an air-cooled engine is extremely expensive and the last thing Volkswagen needed after such heavy investment in the modern passenger cars was a huge bill for developing air-cooled engine technology. There was a much cheaper and more efficient way of doing things.

During the 1950s and 1960s, diesel engines were crude and painfully noisy – Mercedes diesels were a possible exception – but hasty development and improvement saw something of a diesel 'revolution' by the late 1970s. Diesels were not powerful without the later addition of a turbocharger and inter-cooler but with large capacity they gave acceptable performance and were much more economical. After the 1973 Middle East oil crisis when fuel prices escalated, fuel economy had become an important consideration, especially for the operators of commercial vehicles, whose annual fuel bills could be as much as five times higher than the average private Volkswagen owner's.

By the end of the 1970s, the classic air-cooled Wedges had just about reached the end of their lives. When journalists tested them many did so reluctantly and then it was usually a Camper version 'blagged' for the weekend, and they reported what everyone had come to expect. Their stories detailed such qualities as the excellent utilisation of interior space, thoughtful layout of instruments and controls, comfort of the upholstery, 'wandering' in crosswinds, excellent levels of equipment and . . . the huge lack of engine performance.

It is perhaps a sad reflection on the Bus, or perhaps the people employed to write about it, that the editor of British specialist magazine *VW Motoring*, Robin Wager, was the only journalist actually to bother driving one at a Silverstone test day in 1980. On these occasions, manufacturers traditionally provide an assortment of vehicles for assessment by professional commentators. On this occasion, the Wedge Transporter supplied by Volkswagen sat parked in the pit lane, almost unnoticed all day!

All things considered, the Wolfsburg manufacturer had little option but to pursue the orthodox water-cooled-engine route. It made sense because there was no real alternative. *Aficionados*, however, were not pleased when rumours of water-cooled engines became a reality. In 1982, the last of the German-made, air-cooled Wedges halted production. Production of diesel-engined Transporters had begun as early as March 1981, which signalled a change in the company's direction for the future.

By this time Volkswagen had become an important and huge player on the international stage, with business interests on a scale that most people can only imagine. During 1981 alone, the company had signed an agreement for future collaboration with Nissan, half a million Rabbits – the American Golf – had been produced in North America, and they replaced chief executive, Toni Schmucker, with Carl Hahn. Transporters were also being produced in Buenos Aires by the end of the year and, of course, in Mexico the Puebla plant had successfully completed the 20-millionth Beetle. Volkswagen had become the 'new age' global travellers of the automotive world, and bigger than anyone could have envisaged in 1945 when Ivan Hirst was trying to make sense among the rubble and remains of what had been a modern and productive factory.

Few vehicles of the late 1970s were more typically Germanic than a white painted Volkswagen Kombi. Functional and entirely to the point, this 'no-nonsense' people carrier remains just about unsurpassed in its intended role, a facet reflected in the high resale value these Transporters command today.

Developed and changed almost out of recognition, each successive generation was improved in many respects, yet the 'box on wheels' philosophy remained intact throughout. 'Splittie', Bay and Wedge, these vehicles were the first of their kind – the true leaders – and fought off fierce competition from rivals throughout production of all three generations. The 'cult' following that has developed around these vehicles has grown and is understandably bigger than ever.

A vast expanse of wet, grey tarmac sits under a leaden sky, the Wedge Panelvan looking equally austere upon its launch in 1979. In the open position the vast sliding side door and large 'barn door' tailgate illustrate the practicalities of Wedge ownership. A spectacular launch in the south of France amid sunshine and exotic vegetation is favoured by many manufacturers for new vehicles, but Volkswagen rarely need such extravagance. Transporters had little to prove by this stage.

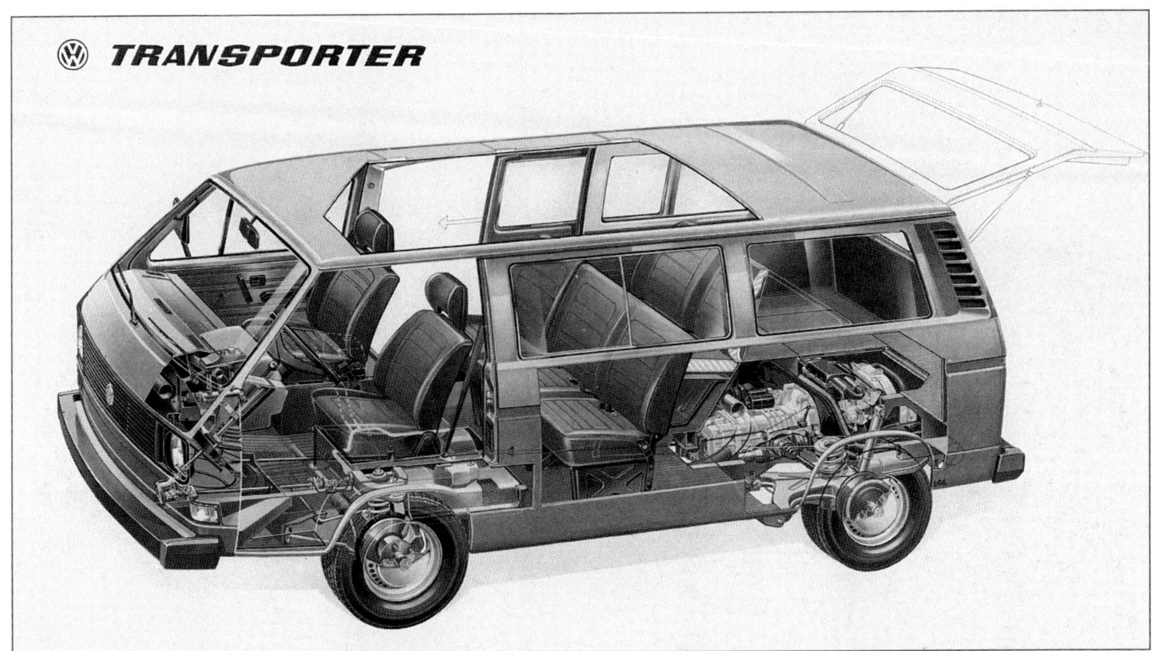

Everything you need to know about the internal secrets of a Wedge Bus – this is state-of-the-art Volkswagen at its best during the 1980s. An eight-seater Kombi with the fuel-injected, 2-litre, 70bhp engine was Hanover's ultimate development of the air-cooled theme. The basic layout remains the same, although purists bemoaned the passing of torsion-bar suspension in favour of coil springs. The spare wheel on this model was tucked out of harm's way in a compartment below the cab floor, which was convenient until it was needed.

The weight of the horizontally opposed, air-cooled, four-cylinder engine and alloy cased gearbox almost perfectly balanced the weight of driver and passengers, but change was afoot at Volkswagen right from the model's inception. Coil springs and wishbone suspension were in keeping with the company's modern passenger saloon range and with undistinguished rivals!

This detail of Volkswagen's transaxle system clearly shows the narrow driveshafts (introduced originally on the Bay), articulated with universal joints and the starter motor and solenoid on the gearbox casing. This layout served Volkswagen well for many years and, in terms of engineering integrity, has never been improved upon since. Later transverse engines driving the front wheels suit manufacturers but many customers remain unconvinced.

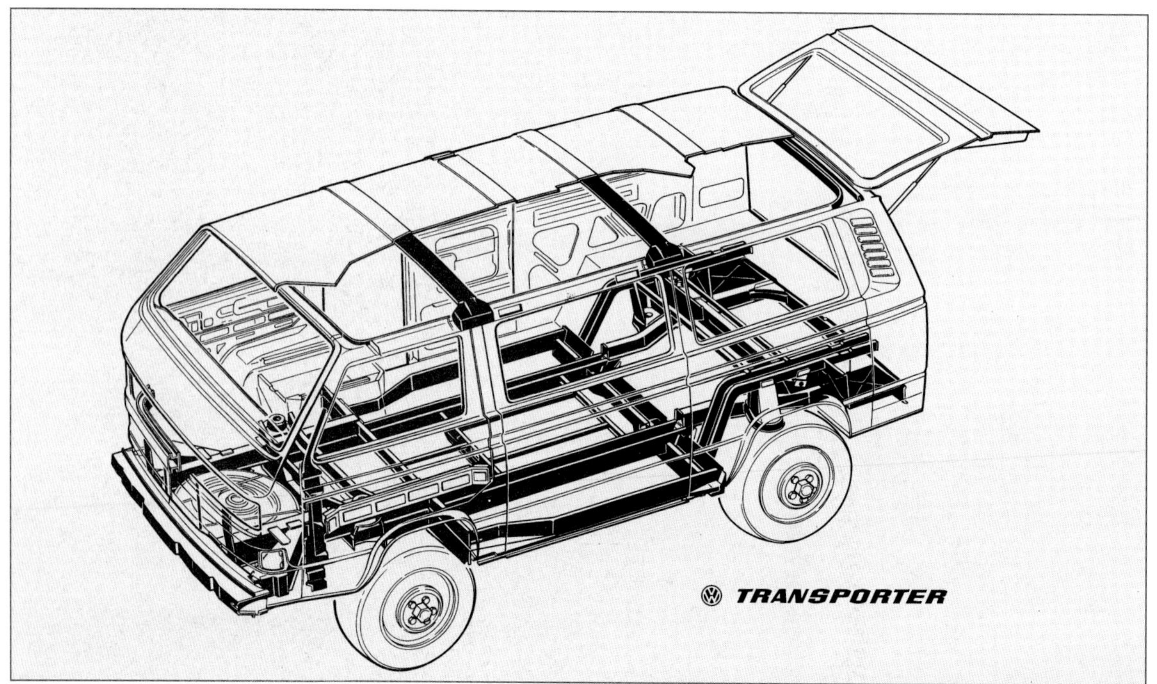


Despite many detail changes and a host of improvements across the board, the Wedge's basic chassis frame configuration had not changed since the 'Splittie' prototypes of 1949. There is a sturdy 'ladder' frame braced with crossmembers and outriggers to support the sills and outer body. These components, constructed from sturdy box sections, were much larger than previously and stronger to cope with the vehicle's weight and size. Note the thickness of the roof hoops.

By the late 1970s the results of crash testing were responsible for much stronger and more complex bodyshells. Apart from front and rear 'crumple zones', there are reinforcing beams in the cab doors and a hefty transverse 'girder' directly behind the front panel. Despite these laudable efforts, motorists continue to have serious accidents. Perhaps future efforts to improve road safety should be centred less on car makers and more on educating road users.

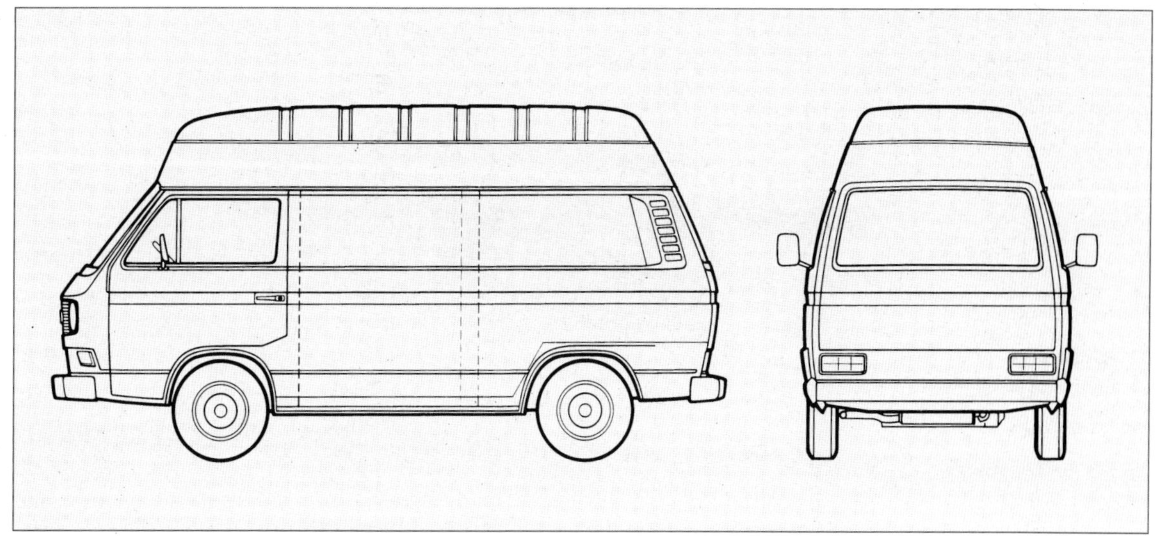

Naturally, the Wedge was available as a High-roof Panelvan with a truly cavernous interior. Just for once, Volkswagen's draughtsmen resisted the urge to splatter this beautifully drawn illustration with meaningless dimensions . . .

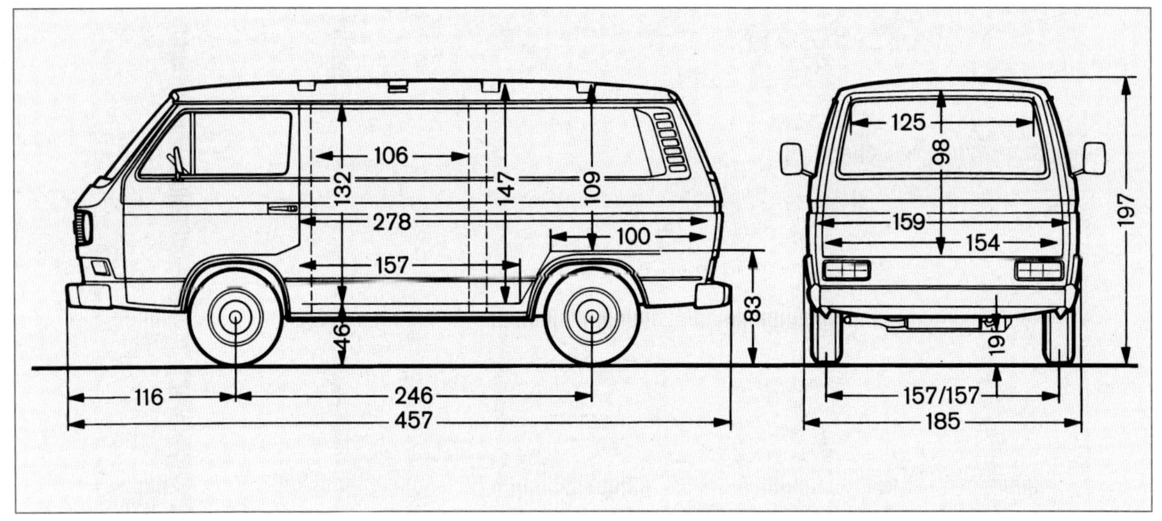


. . . but went full steam ahead where the regular Panelvan was concerned.

The Wedge's huge 'barn door' tailgate, supported on either side by a strut, created easy access to the load area. The only drawback with the rear engine position is that the cargo platform is necessarily higher than that of conventional front-engined vehicles. Front-wheel drive has many disadvantages but, with the engine also in the front, there is at least a lower floor at the rear.

Wedges continued to be built with heavily corrugated floor panels to add strength to the overall body structure. The walkway between the two cab seats had been an option on some 'Splittie' models and standard on most models in the third-generation Wedge. This had always been considered a great advantage, particularly on people carriers, as this facility allowed access to the passengers or contents in the rear.

The last of the classic air-cooled Single- and Double-cab Pick-ups. These vehicles were, and remain, among the most practical of all Transporters, particularly the Double-cabs. Able to seat as many as six, and with the option of a tarpaulin to cover the bed, they were never intended as ideal family transport but more and more are used as such nowadays.

The start of a day's work with just one tray of plants loaded on to the back of a new, pristine 'Pritschenwagen', or Pick-up. Horticulture was but one branch of the German economy that made good use of the new Volkswagen commercials. Incidentally, chromium-plated hubcaps were not available as standard on Pick-ups in all markets; the majority had a brushed satin finish.

Modern, spacious, simple and entirely functional, the Wedge's dashboard, instrumentation, switchgear and controls were well thought out and ergonomically correct. The 'acres' of non-reflecting black plastic covering the dashboard – widely used by most manufacturers during the late 1970s – drew considerable criticism for lacking style, but this continuing vogue is now accepted as part and parcel of interior design. However, modern Alfa Romeos and the new Beetle have done much to reverse this trend, thankfully.

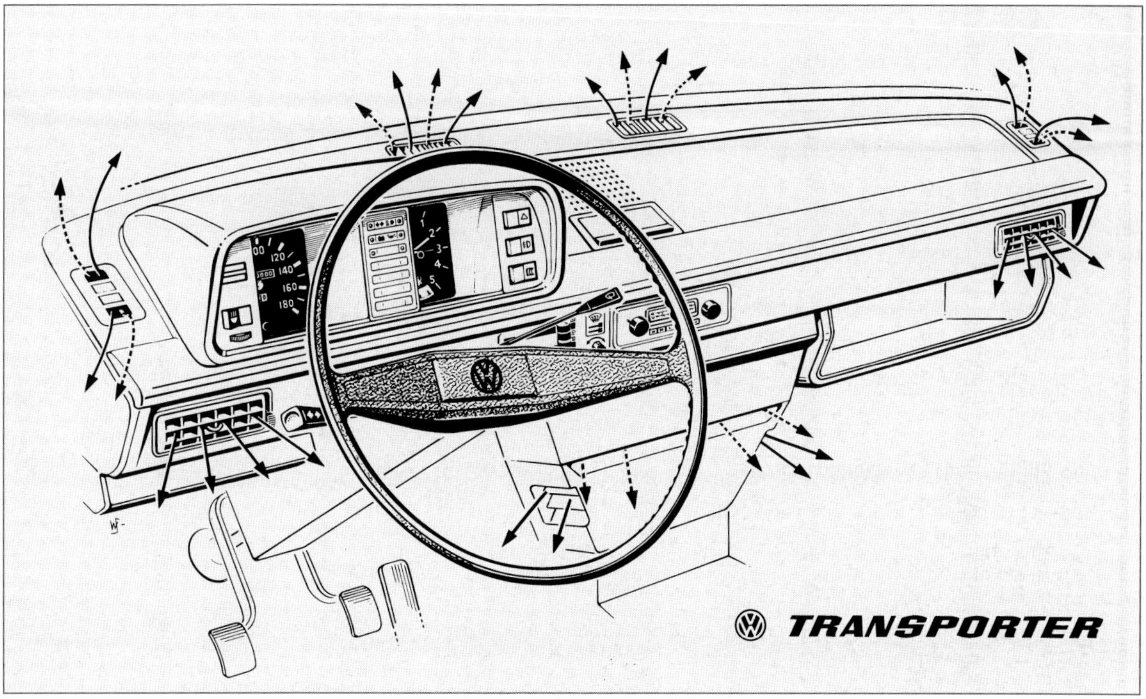

Having been criticised in some quarters for poor interior ventilation of 'Splitties' and Bays, Volkswagen's designers attempted to ensure that they were not censured for the same reason with the Wedge. Both the windscreen and passengers were well served by fresh air, although this was increasingly tainted with exhaust fumes by the early 1980s. Note that the pedals are top-hinged (in contrast to the previous models' bottom-hinged units) and that the steering wheel has very little styling charisma.

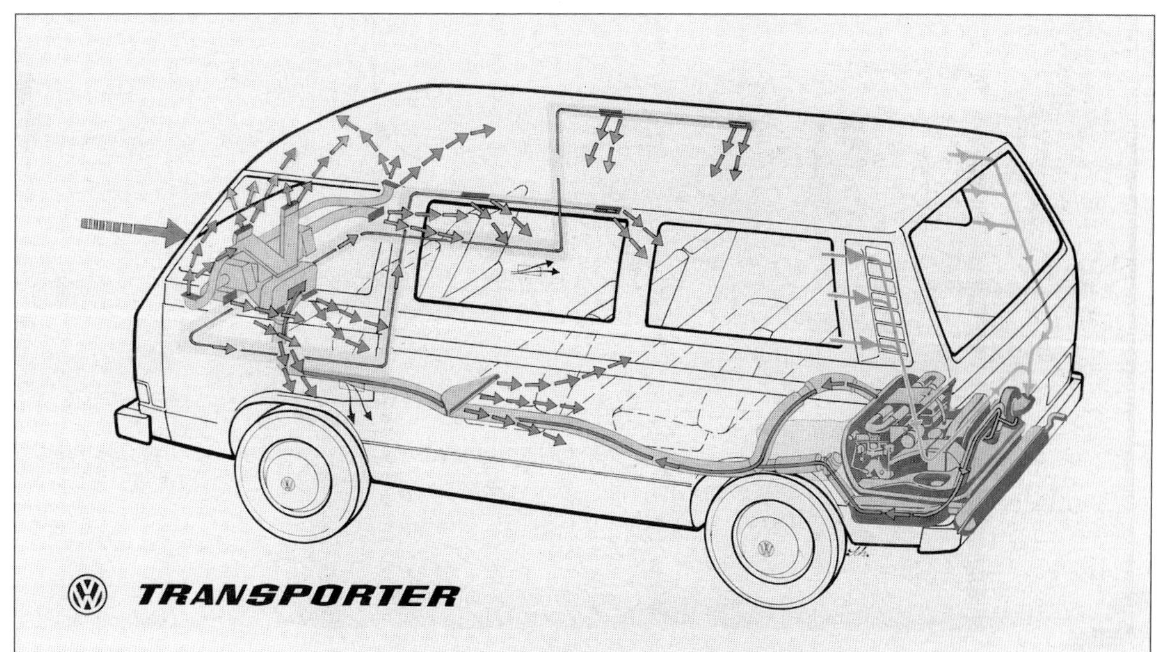



The cabin heating system had not changed in principle in many years. Hot air created by the exhaust system is utilised by a heat-exchanger system – metal cylinders around the exhaust pipes – which is directed through pipes to the interior. Criticism of poor heating has been vociferous in recent times; original equipment exhaust systems made by Volkswagen provide the solution.

Kombis, Pick-ups and Panelvans had cab seating that was as functional – even austere – as ever. The seat covers are in hard-wearing, easy-to-clean vinyl with a 'dog-tooth' pattern but, in contrast to the early 'Splitties', the vehicle benefited from a headlining, head restraints and seat belts. Note that the angle of the steering wheel is more in keeping with the style of a car than in previous years.

As previously, Kombi people carriers doubled as cargo transporters. With the rear seat folded down the huge amount of space appealed to people with large families and taxi drivers alike, but the absence of a full headlining in the Kombi was a bit much for some to accept in the late 1970s.

The Transporter's suitcase engine, access to which was through a removable hatch in the rear luggage panel, was neat and compact, the ancillaries having been moved to much lower positions. This engine saw service in Bays from 1971 but, regrettably, the beauty of the flat-four is completely hidden from view. The distributor, coil, fuel pump and induction system do not exactly make for exciting viewing.

As a family touring vehicle the Wedge was virtually unrivalled in carrying capacity, comfort and practicality. Towards the end of the 1970s, there was no shortage of motorised caravans, either, but the Volkswagen Westfalia conversion remained a firm favourite. In the depths of a dark, dull, English winter, scenes like this of interesting summer holidays touring through the spectacular scenery of mainland Europe in a Kombi, are depressingly tantalising.

Two plus two! Mother and father are on holiday in Lazise, Italy, with the children, who appear to be resisting the prospect of consuming lunch at the Grotta Hotel.

Spacious lay-bys are welcome features on Europe's massive road network. Here, a Wedge rejoins the carriageway to take its place among other classics from the late 1970s. These include a Mk1 Golf, S-Class Mercedes-Benz and Audi 100, exciting cars that are now appreciated for the superb machines that they are. Like these models, the Transporter would develop into a much heavier and flabby machine with a high price tag, high level of electronic sophistication and very little in the way of character.

Sharing a Westfalia Camper with a large, shaggy dog in an empty boatyard is not everyone's idea of fun, but this is what Campers were partially all about. Above all else, these vehicles allowed ordinary people to pursue weekend and holiday interests with complete flexibility, and there was a free bed for the night. Incidentally, it was W.G. Grace who first coined the phrase: 'Anyone who loves whisky and hates dogs can't be all bad.'

Wedges continued in the Transporter's role as a safari vehicle. This is one of the few vehicles of the 1980s that had a genuine use for the most aptly named 'bull' bars. Vehicle designers have worked hard over the years to make their products safer, particularly from a pedestrian's point of view, but these 'cow-catching' irons continue to predominate on macho four-wheel drives.

Regrettably, but understandably, Volkswagen's publicity shots rarely showed a true picture of the Pick-up's role in the building trade. It is more likely that this Pick-up would only resemble a new vehicle for the first hour of its life. From then on it would be grossly overloaded, its paintwork chipped away from its bodywork and the two guys loading would invariably be puffing on a cigarette and cursing and swearing.

Hardwood strips on the Pick-up's bed were designed to prevent loads from slipping and to protect the metal to which they were attached. The utility objects on this bed have been carefully arranged for the purpose of photographic composition – a busy builder would not have been quite so fussy.

This official publicity shot high up on the spectacular Gross Glockner Pass in Austria is profoundly significant and telling of Volkswagen's policy of aiming the Wedge at the better-off. Whereas Bay-window people carriers largely catered for the pockets of younger folk with children, Wedges appealed to richer, older folk who looked forward to holidays without the kids. The man with the pipe, incidentally, is not just a stereotypical figment of the publicity department's imagination: Germans, Austrians and Swiss continue to sport national costume.

The long, demanding climb to the top of the Gross Glockner is one that the owners of some conventional modern vehicles fear, as the latter have a habit of boiling their radiators. This has never been a problem with air-cooled Buses, of course, which is why dozens make this trip over the top of this mountain every summer. This same road was one of Ferdinand Porsche's favourite routes, which he tackled on more than one occasion in a Split-window Beetle.

WOB·SP 99

With a change of clothing the same middle-aged people have arrived in the Dolomite Mountains, Italy. This journey from Germany is a fair distance, yet the Bus is devoid of travel stains. As late as 1979 not even professional photographers had discovered the trick of 'wetting' the tyre walls to artificially enhance the aesthetic appeal of the Bus.

Destination Austria for our intrepid heroes, but never mind the fabulous three-storey house, mountainous background and luscious vegetation and concentrate hard on the Wedge. Clearly visible is the distinctive tread pattern of Michelin XZX radial tyres, which were standard in most markets across the Wedge range. Journalists largely attributed the superior road-holding of these Buses to modern coil-spring suspension but radials provided the real answer.

'Executive' custom conversions proliferated during the Wedge era and were very expensive. Parked next to an aircraft, this is an attempt to portray the average Wedge owner as a prosperous 'jet setter'. Of all the accessories fitted to this vehicle the chin spoiler is the most useful, which helped with aerodynamic stability and negated the Wedge's tendency to 'wander' in crosswinds. It is, however, difficult to appreciate the practical value of convex side windows.

# CHAPTER SIX

# A NEW AGE, 1982–99

*High up in the European alps (as its licence plate suggests), a water-cooled Wedge keeps going in deep snow. The engine might have been water cooled, but it remained in the rear and still provided excellent traction. These vehicles continued to be popular in the hillier parts of Germanic countries for rather obvious reasons.*

# INTRODUCTION

Although the classic and much-loved air-cooled engines had been banished to the annals of Volkswagen lore – and some VW people genuinely considered this as the end of civilisation in its most familiar form – the Wedge Transporter lived on until 1989. To the casual observer, its appearance was the same as ever but there was a significant change to the front panel. This incorporated a wide, black-painted grille, behind which was a water radiator – anathema to Volkswagen *aficionados*. The engine – 'Wasserboxer' as it was dubbed in Germany – was still in the tail but, instead of having cast-iron fins protruding from the cylinder barrels, the 'block' had a smooth alloy finish and was shrouded with water jackets.

Purists scoffed but this 1.9-litre engine was quieter, more powerful and eminently more suited to the age in which it flourished. And while many owners of these vehicles could not speak highly enough of them, sceptics of the 'old school' loved to quote 'horror' stories about the 'Wasserboxer's' inability to travel much beyond 50,000 miles (80,000 km) without developing serious mechanical problems. By and large these stories were to be taken with a pinch of salt.

The 1.6-litre diesel engine was a conventional four-cylinder power unit and developed 50bhp at 4,200rpm, the same output as the Bus's 1600 air-cooled engine. The former was not able to move these vehicles along any more quickly than the air-cooled engine, but it was a good deal more economical, using fuel at an average rate of 35mpg.

The 'Wasserboxer' petrol engine continued to sound like a flat-four but not an air-cooled flat-four. It had something of a muted growl about it that smacked of convention. The Bus was no longer a product of unorthodox thinking, but of a new age in which compliance with the norm became an economic necessity for all manufacturers, including Volkswagen.

Camper manufacturers such as Westfalia, Holdsworth and others loved these Wedges and there was a host of custom builders, who specialised in kitting out their versions with every conceivable modern convenience. There appeared to be no upper limit to the cost of such vehicles, many retailing for the equivalent of an average three-bedroom, semi-detached English house.

Volkswagens were still perceived as the leaders in the Camper market but due to the presence of serious rival manufacturers, they did not enjoy the same niche as they once had. Among Talbots, Fiats, Mercedes and others, the strong Volkswagen Camper image was mingling with the crowds, instead of standing head and shoulders above them.

These vehicles were also well beyond the financial reach of traditional clientele, who looked to the past to fulfill their motoring needs. More and more people began to view 'Splitties' and Bays in a very different light. Even the rustiest, most incomplete hulks were literally dragged from scrapheaps and rebuilt.

As a result of the emergence of an independent industry specialising in spare parts – many of them faithfully reproduced to original patterns – a restoration 'craze' began. In Britain, people like Alan Schofield founded a business building and supplying virtually all components necessary for the restoration of a 'Splittie', Bay and Wedge. Alan is a genuine Volkswagen enthusiast and many an old Bus has survived due to his efforts.

By 1989, the Wedge had survived another decade. This vehicle had enjoyed a relatively long production run but, by the time of its demise, it no longer made sense for Volkswagen to continue with a rear-engined vehicle when the rest of the range had engines mounted up front. Among other things there were accountants carefully watching every item of expenditure, and they introduced a new word, rationalisation, to Anglo-American (not German) vocabulary. Rationalisation had a meaning – cutting costs!

In 1989, a new, fourth-generation Bus was launched with the same models as before, but it was altogether different from anything Volkswagen had produced in the past. It was still a 'box on wheels' – it could not be anything else – but traditional Volkswagen people could not make a lot of sense of it. With front-wheel drive and a range of engines from the 68bhp 1.9-litre turbo-diesel to the 140bhp 2.8-litre V6 petrol engine, these vehicles appealed to a new generation of enthusiasts, while the old one took no notice.

The new Transporters were quiet, fast, comfortable and well equipped in every sense, with state-of-the-art gadgetry employed throughout. Yet, if the V-over-W emblem was removed from the front panel and hind quarters, it was difficult to recognise this Transporter as a Volkswagen.

Incidentally, 'badgeless' Volkswagens were much in evidence in Britain during the early 1990s. A rap band, the Beastie Boys, became popular and whatever the merits of the Beastie Boys' music, their followers – thousands of them – identified themselves more closely with the band by marauding around streets and supermarket car parks for the purpose of removing VW badges from sundry Volkswagens. This craze died down with one extraordinary conclusion, apart from revealing the lack of character and individual identity in so many modern Volkswagens: VAG UK offered owners free replacement badges, which was a small price to pay for the massive amount of free press publicity that the saga had generated.

In the mid-1990s, Volkswagen added yet another string to its MPV bow. Apart from the large LT truck range, which is not discussed here, the people-carrying theme was extended with the release of the Sharan. This vehicle was the result of a joint venture with Ford, and the two companies made the same vehicle but with different badges.

Perhaps understandably in Britain, VAG's marketing department objected vociferously to the name bestowed upon this multi-seated and handsomely styled vehicle. It sounded too similar to a popular girl's name, which had become the butt of a number of exceptionally crude, although extremely funny, jokes. One Volkswagen spokesman told this author that he feared for a follow-up vehicle dubbed 'Tracey', another name that attracted contemporary humorists, but this has yet to happen.

Something of a 'hybrid' between a car and bus, the Sharan follows a well-worn theme that loosely started with Renault's highly acclaimed, plastic-panelled Espace during the mid-1980s. Apart from offering more headroom than a conventional passenger saloon, and not many other advantages besides, these so-called MPVs have become fashionable accoutrements in certain middle-class sectors of European and American society. The Sharan is an 'alternative school-run' vehicle, but in terms of styling and overall appeal, is closer to the original 'Splittie' concept than the large Transporters of the 1990s.

In Brazil the classic air-cooled Bay-window Bus is still in production and continues to sell exceptionally well. A Bristol-based company in England began importing small batches of them during 1998, and there are signs that these will prove popular in this market, nearly twenty years after German production halted.

What the future holds for Volkswagen and its fortunes is anyone's guess. The company's current chairman, Ferdinand Piech, grandson of Professor Ferdinand Porsche, has publicly stated his aim of providing a Volkswagen in virtually every sector of the market, from the Lupo 'minicar' at one end to the W12-engined 'supercar' – still at prototype stage in 1998 – at the other.

A fifth-generation Transporter is inevitable, as are a sixth and seventh. Early signs are that the next, and maybe subsequent Buses, will ape the traditional Split-screen Transporter more closely than the new, front-drive Beetle resembles the traditional rear-engined saloon. It will doubtless have a front-mounted, water-cooled engine driving the front wheels, and perhaps there will be a four-wheel-drive version, but no one really knows.

I anticipate that the next Bus will have eliptical headlamps in the style of the Mercedes-Benz E class and 'Splittie' Bus, a prominent VW roundel in the centre of the front panel and somehow a 'Y' shaped swage line will have been contrived on the nose as well. The road wheels will be 16-in diameter items, as were those fitted to Buses in the early 1950s, the interior will be filled with safety features such as airbags, and the tailgate will be of the barn-door variety. It probably will not sell in such large numbers as the new Beetle but will be every bit as successful as its illustrious forebears.

The new Beetle is built alongside the traditional one at Puebla, Mexico. The former car's future is bright, the latter's uncertain. Rumours have persisted for years that production of the traditional Beetle must be axed one day. If and when it does finally come to an end, it might just be to make way for production of the fifth-generation 'retro-clone' Transporter, which is a most intriguing possibility. The air-cooled rear-engined Beetle is Mexico's cheapest form of motorised four-wheeled transport; employment is also dependent upon its continued production and the Mexican government is very much aware of this. A new Bus produced there would be well beyond the pockets of average Mexicans, which is why the Beetle might well live on.

If new Transporters are made in Hanover, as Transporters have been since 1956, the old Beetle's future is assured for many years. And so is the Bus's. No vehicle in the history of commercials has come close to the achievements of the Volkswagen Transporter. They are unique vehicles and wholly deserving of their classic standing.

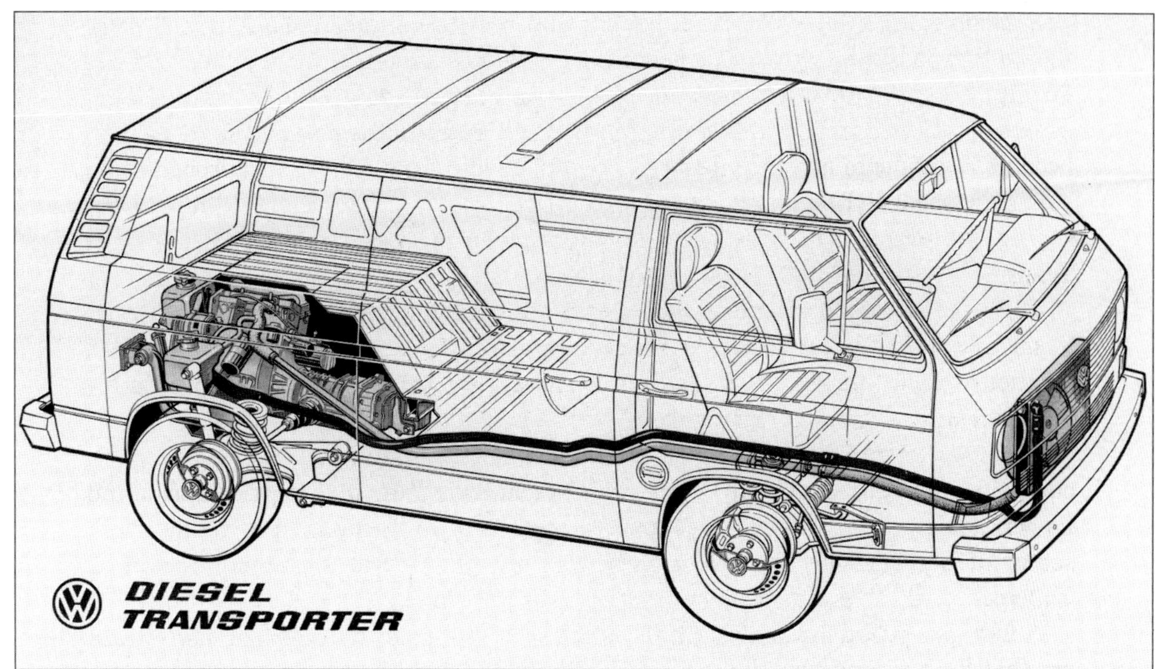


By the mid-1970s the writing was on the wall for under-powered air-cooled engines. The conventional in-line, four-cylinder diesel unit that saw service in the company's other models came into service in 1980 and, although it produced no more power than the traditional air-cooled engine, it was far more economical. The long pipes from front to rear are water conduits to and from the cooling radiator up front – anathema to VW purists.

In Britain and the majority of her Commonwealth countries, the Land Rover remained a best-seller in horse and agricultural circles. In Germanic countries the all-purpose, four-wheel drive Mercedes G-Wagen was not as popular as it might have been and the Wedge Transporter was a logical alternative. It had the added advantage of considerably more interior space.

Expensive, exceptionally well made and fitted with almost every conceivable luxury, the range-topping Caravelle Carat provided real competition for middle-ranking executive saloons. Porsche are reputed to have had one of these vehicles fitted with a 911 turbo engine and the interior kitted out for high-speed boardroom meetings!

A Caravelle with 'chauffeur' at the wheel and mum and dad and their two kids beautifully groomed, crisply dressed and ready to go precisely nowhere. This is yet another posed studio publicity shot that illustrates as much about the media's stereotyping of an 'average' family in the 1980s as it does about the comfort and practical value of a Caravelle. In the style of all traditional 'minibus' drivers, this one has naturally adopted the pursed lips of someone who is well used to aimlessly whistling irritating 'tunes'. A safe and luxurious motoring environment, the range-topping Microbus has plush upholstery, seat belts and head restraints to minimise the possibility of 'whiplash' in the event of an accident.

The Caravelle's velour covered seats – not particularly easy to clean – fold to produce a couple of useful beds. This was particularly important for business users covering vast mileages in Europe.

The Double-cab Pick-up seeks to prove that it is perfectly capable of pulling a trailer neatly loaded with a Ransomes mowing machine. However, with a solitary chap in the six-seater cab and the Pick-up's bed completely empty, this is a solid example of Volkswagen's publicity people missing the point by quite some margin.

The superb and tremendously useful four-wheel-drive Syncro Wedge became available in the 1980s. This system operated in rear-drive mode in normal conditions, with the front wheels engaging drive automatically when electronic 'gizmos' detected a loss in traction. Had Volkswagen taken Ferry Porsche's advice, a four-wheel-drive would have been produced several years earlier.

A Syncro 'Werkstattwagen' specially kitted out with storage cupboards, circular saw, overhead drill, vice and workbench – what an amateur DIY enthusiast would not give to demonstrate his lack of skill with a cache like this!

As the registration number suggests, there is quite a gap between the front wheel and the ground in one of Volkswagen's many attempts to illustrate the Syncro's extraordinary off-road ability. This vehicle – a pristine Pick-up – is actually stationary and posing nicely for the camera. This model was among the best and most practical of all VW Transporters.

Rallies for four-wheel-drive vehicles have become increasingly popular in recent years, the Paris–Dakar event being the most dangerous and demanding. Here a Double-cab Syncro gets the 'thumbs-up', much to the rather obvious relief of the driver.



It is doubtful whether a zebra would be fooled into sending out a mating call to this striped breed of animal, but at least this Syncro has sufficient power and grip to beat a hasty retreat if one were to.

Very much in the 'Lichtenheit' style of the Mercedes-Benz SLs of the late 1950s and 1960s, the stacked headlamps were popular conversions in Germany. This was not just an attempt at vehicle personalisation but a laudable means of increasing the vehicle's powers of illumination, which were never among Volkswagen's 'brighter' ideas.

History repeating itself and having an effect many years ahead! Apart from the large 'barn door' tailgate, the English word 'Weekender' (the use of which has been outlawed in France), appears as a model designation on the rear. Not too many English vehicles have German names, although Rolls-Royce once launched a car in Germany as the Silver Mist without realising that mist in German means 'dung heap'. Enough said.

VW customising became lucrative business in the 1980s. This example sports singularly unattractive alloy wheels, distinctive 'racing' style cooling ducts and a custom high-roof, sloped at the front at the same angle as the windscreen. Body graphics were then in infancy.

When diesel-engined Wedges were additionally fitted with a turbocharger they became powerful as well as economical. This is one of many versions with a special box body.

A comfortable fully equipped mobile office with computer, fax machine and telephone; despite these wonders of modern technology – fine when they work properly – there is a relic from the old world, a ballpoint pen, on the table.

VAG UK's marketing people were not happy with the Sharan appellation but this gorgeous-looking MPV, developed in collaboration with Ford, is much closer to the original people carriers of the 1950s than the contemporary Transporter. The additional headroom provided by this type of vehi-

cle is, of course, pointless but an increasing trend on which Volkswagen would have been foolish not to capitalise.

After the Wedge came the Type 4 Transporter, which was larger, generally more expensive, much better equipped and a good deal more powerful. However, on the other side, it had front-wheel drive, which doubtless cut production costs, and conventional, characterless styling. Traditional enthusiasts turned their backs on these vehicles. Remove the VW roundel from the radiator grille and this could be a Fiat, Peugeot, Toyota or anything else from 'mainstream' manufacturers.

This amazingly safe vehicle – all-round visibility is first class – and built to VW's uncompromising standards but the alloy wheels and colour-coded Kamei body kit do little to disguise the rather ordinary nature of the vehicle. Trapped by the fashionable ugliness and design uniformity of the 1990s, these Transporters will probably never be regarded as classics; Volkswagen will have to be more creative than this if the company's reputation for building individualist's vehicles is to remain intact.

The 1990s Pick-up truck with a cab that is out of proportion with the all-important bed. With a full load at the rear and the driving wheels at the front, traction on loose or slippery surfaces is virtually non-existent, which defeats the object of the original Bus concept.

The classic Transporters with their rear-mounted, air-cooled engines took a final bow in 1982. These vehicles form the basis of the Transporter 'cult'. Practical considerations and styling alone justify true classic status; their like will be seen again. The trend towards 'retro' styling across the motor industry will ensure that features of a past age will return during the course of the twenty-first century.

# INDEX